Additional Praise for
Teachers with the Courage to Give

"I want us to think about a curriculum of care the same way we
would think about the math or language curriculum—it's impossible to imagine a school without it. In this book,
Jackie Waldman brings us stories of teachers who are
making a curriculum of care a reality every day."

–HAROLD BRATHWAITE, Director of Education,
Peel District School Board, Ontario, Canada

"Reading this book had me reaching for the tissue box,
laughing out loud, and sending up prayers of thanks for the
good teachers in my own life. Bless 'em all and bless
Jackie Waldman for giving teachers these pages
to tell you their stories."

–ANN MEDLOCK, President,
The Giraffe Heroes Project

Praise for
The Courage to Give

"Reminds us that our true purpose is to serve
each other, regardless."

–WALLY "FAMOUS AMOS," author of *The Power in You*

"*The Courage to Give* offers readers true inspiring stories
that remind us there is always a silver lining."

–ARIELLE FORD, author of
Hot Chocolate for the Mystical Soul

Praise for
Teens with the Courage to Give

"Inspirational true tales that make you want to get out and give!"

—MIAMI HERALD

"The examples set by the contributors, together with the follow-up contacts, will help empower other readers to improve themselves and the world."

—BOOKLIST

"These inspiring teens show us that by giving to others, we realize our best selves. Jackie Waldman has written a deeply moving book about the power of young people to change the world."

—ANDREW SHUE, actor and co-founder of Do Something

TEACHERS *with the*
Courage *to* Give

Everyday Heroes
Making a Difference
in our Classrooms

Edited by Jackie Waldman

Foreword by Bob Chase,
President, National Education Association

CONARI PRESS
Berkeley, California

Conari Press books are distributed by Publishers Group West.

Cover Photography: © Getty Images, Inc., Stephen Stickler
Cover and Book Design: Suzanne Albertson

Library of Congress Cataloging-in-Publication Data
Teachers with the courage to give / edited by Jackie Waldman.
p.   cm.
Includes bibliographical references.
ISBN 1-57324-758-8
1. Teachers—United States—Case studies. 2. Teachers—Canada—Case studies.
3. Effective teaching—Case studies. I. Waldman, Jackie.
LB1775.2 .T464 2002
371.1'00973—dc21   2002000349

Printed in the United States of America.

02 03 04 05   RRD NW   10 9 8 7 6 5 4 3 2 1

*To every teacher we have
encountered—in a classroom or
just along the way—who has shared
knowledge and wisdom, believed
in our potential, and ignited
our spark of kindness, truth,
and uniqueness.*

I touch the future; I teach.

—Christa McAuliffe

TEACHERS with the Courage to Give

T hroughout my twenty-six years in the classroom and more recently as president of NEA, I have always been amazed by the high caliber of people who choose the teaching profession—a career without rank, riches, or fame. Clearly, teachers have a special motivation: They are committed to making a difference in the lives of children.

That is why most people can recall at least one teacher who played a critical role in their lives. Recalling his teenage years, musician Carlos Santana recounts how one of his teachers put him on the path to his musical career:

"Mr. Knudsen was special to me because he knew something I didn't know about myself." The teacher recognized his talents both as an artist and a musician, and convinced the boy to choose one or the other "and give it 100 percent."

"When he told me that, I started crying. I had never had anyone care about me as a person," Santana relates.

In *Teachers with the Courage to Give*, dozens of educators working in America's public school classrooms share their own stories of small miracles and great teaching moments. They are uplifting stories that remind us how one teacher can impact a child's life. They are powerful stories that make us believe that every student has a unique contribution to offer the world. They are inspiring stories of teachers who can ignite the spark of enlightenment and cultivate minds. They are heartwarming stories that honor the everyday heroes who daily give of themselves to their students.

And they are personal stories that can give all teachers a sense of connection, support, and affirmation.

These remarkable narratives show us the personal and professional fulfillment that comes from giving the ultimate gift: the gift of ourselves.

Dana Moore

No matter what accomplishments you achieve,
somebody helped you.

–Althea Gibson

When I began this book, I asked Cathy Priest, the 1996 Ohio Teacher of the Year, to contribute a great teaching moment— when she touched the life of a student and a student touched hers. Instead, she felt compelled to share with me this experience:

I began my teaching career once my own children started school. That was in 1985. I was the first woman to be hired as a social studies teacher in a rather old, well-established school system in central Ohio. In the fall of 1991, I attended a workshop offered by the local cable company to introduce cable into the classroom. I was one of only four teachers who stayed to find out more about programming that would benefit my social studies classroom. The cable representative and I had a lengthy conversation, and she promised to share with me materials that might benefit my students.

She also introduced to me a Discovery Channel-sponsored contest called "Cultural Safari." While the contest seemed interesting, it was not something I could fit into my curriculum. I was encouraged, however, to challenge students to participate in the contest as an extracurricular project, and they took me up on it to great success. My team of seniors took second place regionally to my team of juniors, and in February 1992, I was notified that my student team had won the national championship. As champions, we were rewarded with a safari to Tanzania.

Once we arrived in Tanzania and I was introduced to our Tanzanian guides, Willie and Gabra, as the teacher, I became the recipient of special treatment. It was not that I was the lone professional with three teenage girls; included in our group were doctors, government officials, and corporate executives. But it was the teacher who got priority attention, whether meal-time (first to be served and graciously offered seconds), shower time (hot water being a premium when heated by campfire), and nap/bedtime (tent quarters with added comforts).

The attention I received made me strangely uncomfortable. Most teachers would understand this. Four days into the safari, I asked Gabra why I had been singled out. He was incredulous that I had asked the question, explaining that my profession "signified" my importance. In his country, "Children are our most precious possessions; and the teachers who shape their future the most valued resources." To be made fully aware of the value with which I was held by these people changed me forever. That evening, on the Serengeti Plain, was the first time I knew pride in my profession, that I did not need to explain the choice I had made to spend my days with teenagers, as their teacher and mentor. Teachers are driven with a purpose that, strangely enough, goes unappreciated in our society. Personally, I cannot imagine where I would be today without the teachers I've had in my life.

When I heard Cathy's story, I was saddened. For an American teacher to have to travel to Africa to first feel honor and pride as a teacher is an embarrassment. We advocate for the need to invest in our children's future, to give each child the potential to become successful, but why don't we take steps to make teaching the most valued profession a person can choose? Aren't our teachers our real heroes?

After having the privilege, as the author of *The Courage to Give* and *Teens with the Courage to Give*, of meeting many teachers who have devoted their lives to our children, I wanted to share their stories, so that we are reminded of just what real heroes they are.

In response to my request for stories about teachers with the courage to give, I received an anonymous e-mail—detailing some of our heroic teachers:

You want heroes?

Consider Dave Sanders, the schoolteacher shot to death while trying to shield his students from two neo-Nazi youth on a bombing and shooting rampage at Columbine High School.

You want heroes?

For Ronnie Holuby, a Fort Gibson, Oklahoma, middle school teacher, it was a routine school day until gunfire erupted. He opened a door to the schoolyard and two students fled past him. A thirteen-year-old student had shot five other students when Holuby stepped outside, walking deliberately toward the boy, telling him to hand over the gun. He kept walking. Finally the boy handed him the gun. Holuby walked the boy to the side of the building, and then sought to help a wounded girl.

You want heroes?

Jane Smith, a Fayetteville, North Carolina, teacher, was moved by the plight of one of her students, a boy dying for want of a kidney transplant. So this white woman told the family of this fourteen-year-old black boy that she would give him one of her kidneys. And she did.

You want heroes?

Doris Dillon dreamed all her life of being a teacher. She not only made it, but she was one of those wondrous teachers who could wring the best out of every single child. One of her fellow teachers in San Jose, California, said, "She could teach a rock to read." Suddenly she was stricken with Lou Gehrig's disease, which is always fatal, usually within five years.

She asked to stay on the job—and did. When her voice was affected, she communicated by computer. Did she go home? She is now running two elementary school libraries. When the disease was diagnosed, she wrote the staff and all the families that she had one last lesson to teach: that dying is part of living. Her colleagues named her Teacher of the Year.

You want heroes?

Last year the average public school teacher spent $468 of her or his own money for student necessities—workbooks, books, pencils, etc.—supplies kids had to have but could not afford. That's a lot of money from the pockets of the most poorly paid teachers in the industrial world.

You want heroes?

The average teacher works more hours in nine months than the average forty-hour employee does in a year.

You want heroes?

For millions of kids, the hug they get from a teacher is the only hug they will get that day. This nation is living through the worst parenting in history. A Michigan principal moved me to tears with the story of her attempt to rescue a badly abused little boy who doted on a stuffed animal on her desk, one that said, "I love you!" He said he'd never been told that at home.

You want heroes?

Despite the problems, public school teachers laugh often. They have the respect of intelligent people and the affection of students who care.

Teachers strive to find the best in their students, even where some see little hope. No other American bestows a finer gift than teaching—reaching out to the brilliant and the retarded, the gifted and the average.

Teachers leave the world a little bit better than they found it. They are America's unsung heroes.

That e-mail led me to many of the remarkable people you will meet in this book. You will meet current and retired teachers who reveal the essence of a great teaching moment—for both teacher and student. You'll meet men and women with the courage to step out of their own lives and step into the lives of their students every single day. You will meet people like Trish Hill, a teacher from Ft. Worth, Texas, who underwent radiation and chemotherapy without missing a day of school because her first graders gave her energy and courage, and Alison Frost, a drama teacher in Houston, who makes casting decisions knowing that the role may be better for the student than the student is for the role. You'll meet Francis Mustapha, a teacher born in a small village in Africa, who teaches in Ft. Wayne, Indiana, and used a student's suicide to create an opportunity for other students to succeed. You'll meet Pam Schmidt, a teacher in Aurora, Colorado, who uses snakes to slither into children's hearts, and Robin Zeal, a teacher in Whitefish, Montana, who received a first grader's mom's wedding ring in hopes she would replace his mom, who recently left his dad and the children.

In his story, Bob Coleman, a retired teacher and National Teachers Hall of Fame inductee in 1994, reminds us of the old story about the frog:

I'm sure you remember it. The frog was once a handsome prince whom a wicked witch turned into an ugly wart-covered creature. Only the kiss of a beautiful maiden could change him back. So there he sat, an unkissed prince trapped inside a frog. But in children's stories and in teaching, miracles do happen. One day a beautiful maiden grabbed up the frog and planted a huge smack right on his lips. Suddenly he was a handsome prince again. And you know the rest—they lived happily ever after.

That is what teaching is all about. We are part of that miracle.

Personally, I learned Bob's lesson the hard way. I'll always remember my first day as a special needs teacher at a high-risk elementary school in a big city. The bulletin boards were filled with posters and charts I had spent days making. The desks had been arranged and rearranged to best accommodate my class of twelve.

Then the bell rang. The children slowly came into the room, checking out the room and me. Suddenly, one ten-year-old ran into the room, took one look at me, ripped down the posters and charts, turned over every desk, and ran out of the room. I followed him. He started running down the stairs and took off, running out of the building and down the street.

After chasing him for a mile and knowing there was no way I could catch up, I stopped. Crying, I returned to school and told my principal my student ran away. While I was speaking with the principal, Jason walked in. Looking at me, he smiled the biggest smile I've ever seen. At that moment I knew he was testing me, waiting to see how I was going to react. A beat of silence followed. I then said, "Jason, will you show me a better way to organize the room?"

Jason gave me a great gift early on in my teaching career—that teaching is about both the student and teacher learning together, and that's when miracles occur. Jason became my best student ever, advancing three reading levels and becoming class leader.

Soon I felt that the four walls of my classroom were too confining. I wanted to teach on a bigger level. Much later, when Conari Press gave me the opportunity to compile *Teachers with the Courage to Give,* I marveled at how serendipitous life can be. But after reading hundreds of powerful stories from teachers across the country and Canada, I realize that I have become the student, learning more than I could ever begin to teach.

We should embrace these teachers' lessons, learn from them, and take them out of the classroom into our own lives. What better way to honor our teachers and our children? An esteemed author and my brilliant editor, M. J. Ryan, asks in *Attitudes of Gratitude,*

Who have you most learned from in your life? Your fourth-grade teacher? A college professor? Your spouse? A therapist or friend? All of the above? Maybe your greatest teachers were those who provided a negative example or provided a mighty obstacle to rebel against. Acknowledging the help we received along the way in our lives—no matter what form it came in—will allow our hearts to soar like a well-tuned orchestra instead of a lonely violin. When we take the time to appreciate those who have been our greatest teachers, we not only express our thanks for the learning but also feel more connected to life as a whole. We see that our lives are a journey on which we become more and more fully who we are meant to be, and that we are helped on our path by a variety of people and circumstances.

In these stories we learn the value of being of service to those who will create the future, of opening our hearts to children, no matter what our own circumstances may be, of seeing beyond a child's actions, loving a child through a personal crisis, and knowing how to listen. Whether we teach school to, parent, befriend, or have chance encounters with a child, we can learn from these teachers what it takes to prepare children for life. While every teacher is called by his or her true name in the stories, I have changed all students' names to protect their anonymity.

Each of us remembers the teacher who made a difference in our life—that special person who gave us a glimpse of what we may accomplish or who we may become. Perhaps that teacher gave us a new perspective on life, on ourselves. The teachers who contributed to this book have certainly touched us. Thanks to each and every one of you for teaching us, through your powerful messages, how to become better people and how possible and critical it is to touch the heart and mind of every child. By honoring teachers, and learning their lessons, we will co-create a safer, kinder world.

My hope is that you will learn from these teachers' contributions what I have—to honor the teachers in our children's lives and in our own, and more specifically, to take the time to express gratitude to the teachers we encounter daily.

So now, I invite you to meet these people and see for yourself the miracles that manifest when we have the courage to give.

CHAPTER 1

Daniel Reynolds, 2000

sLithering into a chiLd's heart

Pam Schmidt

Thunder Ridge Middle School
Aurora, Colorado

'm running a little late. The kids are already here at my classroom door, waiting to get in to take care of the snakes. Lots of chatter and laughter. Searching for my keys, I nearly throw off the delicate balance of my bags of books and papers. A usual Friday morning so far!

Finally I get the door open, and we swirl into the room, the kids all dashing for their favorite snakes. The kids are good about taking care of all of our thirty-eight snakes, but each seems to have a favorite. Some of these young caretakers are kids who gained an interest in snakes through my enrichment mini-course called "Slithers." Others are kids who are in my regular science classes. Still others are kids I've never had in class but who applied for caretaker positions when I "advertised" in the school announcements. My caretakers are a diverse bunch of kids—timid sixth graders, silly seventh graders, and cool eighth graders. We have kids who are part of the "in crowd" and kids who have no crowd at all; very good students and average students and students who have never earned higher than a D; kids who love school and kids who only come to school because of their "snake job." But here, in this classroom, with these snakes, they all belong. They are a cohesive group with a common mission. Each child has important responsibilities and knows that others are depending on him or her to fulfill those responsibilities.

I am busy with the early morning before-class duties—as routine as anything can get in the hormone-heavy halls of a middle school. Writing the day's activities on the chalkboard, accepting some late papers, settling a dispute on whose turn it is to clean that really poopy cage, getting out some more materials for today's lab, helping my teammate's substitute find seating charts, and administering medicine to one of our ailing snakes.

Among all the other talking, squealing, laughing, and jabbering, I hear a heartbreaking cry of distress. Everything else becomes secondary—someone or something is hurting. As I rush across the room, I can tell that something has happened to Cherokee, our beloved Eastern hognose snake that we rescued some years ago from certain starvation. Getting closer, I can see Cherokee's glossy black body sprawled stiffly across his cage floor. He is obviously dead, and it doesn't take much work to figure out what happened. Cherokee still has a partially regurgitated frog lodged in his throat. Something caused him to throw up his food and he asphyxiated. It happened during the night so no one was around to help him.

This is our first totally unexpected death, and the kids don't know how to react. How should they express their shock, their grief? Just then, I look across the table at Rachel. As our eyes meet, her face begins to crumple.

You see, Rachel is having a very rough week. Her grandfather, with whom she had been very close, has recently died. Her entire family was supposed to have driven back for the funeral, to Iowa, I believe. But, a couple days ago we had a terrible snowstorm, so Rachel's mom flew back alone. Rachel has been putting up a brave front for two days now, but this is more than her little heart can take. Bursting into tears, she sobs over this brutal twist of fate with Cherokee, for her mother who traveled to the funeral alone, and for her lost grandfather. My tears are not far behind. As I hold Rachel in my arms, we become enveloped in the arms of the other caretakers, tears in their eyes as well. By our crying, Rachel and mine, we have given the rest of the kids permission to express their grief openly.

We all had a good cry that morning. Then we were able to do what needed to be done to take care of Cherokee's body, to finish up with the other snakes, and to carry on with the rest of the day. We were able to do these things because we were there for each other.

Cherokee's death sent ripples out to the larger school community. Many hearts were touched that day. Many of the teachers and parents finally realized that a snake could be just as meaningful in a child's life as a dog or a cat. People finally saw our snakes as I see them, not just as interesting creatures, but as the tools with which I reach otherwise unreachable children.

Snakes are one of my passions, along with fossils and rocks and rainforests, and many things "scientific." I share my passions with my students, and they join me in the excitement of learning about these things. No, they are not all going to grow up to be herpetologists, paleontologists, or scientists of any kind. But my kids will remember the enthusiasm we shared—and maybe, just maybe, they will take that passion for learning and caring into their future endeavors. It's that very possibility that makes this career worthwhile.

CHAPTER 2

Don Rosner

the power of a smile

Carol Rosner

**Nassau County BOCES
(Board of Cooperative Education)**
Bellmore, New York

've been a teacher of the deaf and hard-of-hearing for more than thirty years. It was not where I had envisioned being, but the opportunity to have the government pay for my master's degree was an opportunity I could not afford to pass up. In all my years of teaching, many special students and their families have touched my life. A few have touched my soul.

Perhaps the one student who stands out above all the rest is Eddie. Eddie is a multiple-handicapped young man who became my student at age twelve. In addition to being deaf, he has cerebral palsy and had a tracheotomy because of early breathing problems. He needed a wheelchair, and it took quite a while to find the proper school to meet all his needs. Eventually, Eddie was placed at our school with a full-time nurse, speech therapist, occupational therapist, physical therapist, and me!

I'll never forget the first time I laid eyes on him. He was an incredibly happy, handsome youngster with the warmest smile I had ever seen. I remember thinking that if anyone were to take away that most remarkable smile they would have to answer to me. Together we shared a remarkable journey. It might help the reader to understand that Eddie was one of a set of twins. At birth his older brother was delivered just fine, but Eddie's delivery was more complicated. Eddie was blessed with an extremely supportive family who were determined to do everything in their power to expose him to the widest degree of stimulation possible.

In Eddie's school, all the students were very needy, and Eddie's grimaces and spastic movements kept people away. His speech was unintelligible, and he knew little sign language. We started to work on sign language, including those words that were helpful with his daily skills. Soon Eddie wanted to learn about everything!

We started to follow current affairs and local news. He wanted names for all the people in his school and what their jobs were. He needed to know about me and my family and what we did. And so it went and so it grew. Then came the computer. Suddenly a way existed for Eddie to explore the world independently. Despite his spastic movements, he was able to steady his hand enough to use the keyboard. We started with the simple language programs and games he could just have fun with.

At this point I wanted to get the people in Eddie's school to interact with him. So I decided to put a word with the corresponding hand-sign on the back of his wheelchair, with an invitation to "stop and learn the sign of the day." A large "happy face" accompanied the announcement. Initially, people were not sure what to make of us. But, slowly, their curiosity encouraged them to inquire about what was going on, and the connection was made. Suddenly, people began to communicate with him and be enchanted by his contagious smile. Eddie became the hot ticket in school! His wonderful smile lit the building. People who had been afraid to talk to him now sought him out. He wasn't so scary—in fact, he was really nice when they gave him a chance.

Eddie's pleasure grew as he became more accepted and connected to his peers. As a teen, he was very age-appropriate in his need for acceptance and social skills. He liked pretty girls and attended all the school dances and other activities. At the age of eighteen he graduated, and I was among those who clapped furiously and cried a lot.

Today, Eddie participates in a day program with some vocational training. He has a girlfriend and aspires to all the things to which most youths aspire.

Whenever I am down, or feeling sorry for myself, I only have to think about Eddie and what he has to deal with on a daily basis. If he can smile, then I certainly can.

Motophoto, 1999

The Doer of Good Becomes Good

Ron Poplau

Shawnee Mission Northwest High School
Shawnee Mission, Kansas

The school administration assured me that my new Community Service class would "make" even though enrollment was low. "Summer transfers will fill the class," the associate principal promised. This was going to be a class like no other—the dream of my career! It would be based totally on a student's trust and initiative; I'd be taking students out of the building and into the community for an hour a day, with special projects in the evening and on weekends. To my dismay, only four students met me on that first fall Monday. Wendy, unfortunately, was one of them. "No way can we have this class with so few students," I said in a defeated tone. Wendy, reeking of cigarette smoke, with unkempt hair and torn jeans, confronted my disappointment with the promise that she would get a roomful of students for me in just three days. Her reputation as a drug addict preceded her, and I could only imagine whom she would attract; after all she had floundered miserably for three years until finally dropping out completely. She had returned this year only to please her father.

You can imagine my utter astonishment when, by Thursday, she had recruited thirteen more students—problem-free and eager to build the new class. It was obvious Wendy was a force with which to be reckoned.

Wendy's story was all too familiar: This once-gifted child's world had been shattered by her parent's divorce, for which she blamed herself—and pot, acid, and Ecstasy filled in the hurt. Even changing school districts and a diminished daily schedule did not help. For a while Wendy would sneak out of her home nightly to rendezvous with fellow "druggies." Her mom would set her alarm clock for every two hours to check on her and, not finding her in bed, would frantically search, find her somewhere in the city, and retrieve her from certain disaster.

Where could I possibly send Wendy? Who would open their door to such a disturbed child? Now that I had the class, could I risk it all? Could Wendy be trusted?

At Wendy's insistence, we put an advertisement in the local paper listing our services, which were free. Suddenly, like the proverbial "big bite" for a fisherman, one family requested assistance, and then others followed suit. There was no denying that this was Wendy's class, and she led the other sixteen. She found plumbers who donated their services; money for utility bills appeared after numerous calls from Wendy. She single-handedly turned this class on and turned her life around. She began to give things away from her own home to folks in need. "I almost had to tie the refrigerator down," her mother told me. "Wendy wanted to give it away. But how could I say No; I was getting my child back. I had been praying for this moment. Her grades started to rise, her attendance was almost perfect, her drug use ceased!"

To the amazement of everyone, this young lady of privilege, whose only concern for months had been taking drugs, began to sit on dirty floors, fight off cockroaches, and spend hours with numerous less fortunate families. Suddenly it was other people's well-being that mattered more that anything else to her. To top it all off, she even chose the class motto: "The Doer of Good Becomes Good!"

Choices had to be made: the prom or a crucial speaking engagement. It took only minutes for Wendy to choose the speaking engagement.

The yearlong class itself did not go unnoticed or unappreciated. Soon came award nominations: Prudential, Noxzema, the *Kansas City Star,* Kiwanis, Optimist, Sertoma.s Even J. C. Penney nominated the class for its Golden Rule Award.

Flanked by the principal, the class sponsor, and Wendy's doting mother, I listened as the awards were presented. When our class was chosen for the first prize, I said to Wendy, "You go up with the principal; it's your award." Wendy rose, shoulders back, and acknowledged the standing ovation. Mom was in tears as she witnessed the transformation of her daughter.

Suddenly, graduation was a mere month away, and students were encouraged to sign up to speak at the evening ceremony. To the surprise of many, Wendy was first on the list. On the evening of graduation, Wendy rose to address a crowd of 6,000 people. Five minutes of sheer eloquence mesmerized the packed house. Her metamorphosis was complete—the doer of good had become good! That night as I prepared for bed I thanked God, for the class had changed Wendy and so many others. Wendy learned the simple lesson that what we do for others comes back more than a hundredfold. Now she would live life to the fullest.

Over at Wendy's house, her mother's alarm clock was not set for the usual two-hour check. It never would be again.

CHAPTER 4

Heddy Bergsman, 2000

Real strength

Chris Pendergast

Dickenson Avenue Elementary
East Northport, New York

'd always thought myself to be a decent teacher. I loved my work and threw myself into it. For twenty-three years, I crafted my trade and honed my skills. By age forty-four, I was a seasoned and competent educator. Life, both personal and professional, had developed a rich fullness, like a ripening fruit in the warmth of summer's sun. Then, on a dank, drizzling October eve, a call came from my neurologist, a call that made my world implode. "I am sorry to tell you, but you have ALS." ALS (also known as Lou Gehrig's disease) is a rapidly progressing neuromuscular disease with no known cause, treatment, or cure. It runs its nasty, paralyzing course in an average of a brief two to three years. I was sentenced to die.

The first of many choices I faced was how I wanted to spend the rest of my life. It was not exactly a yes/no question. Quite early, I made my decision. My life was good. I wouldn't change a thing. In spite of the challenges to come, I knew I wanted to continue teaching.

Little did I realize that this darkest hour would produce my brightest moments. As I began to publicly battle ALS, my class, my school, and my district became my allies as I shifted from teacher to learner, from leader to explorer. We all became a team, learning life's important lessons together.

Part of my teaching assignment in the gifted and talented program is the operation of a mini–nature center called the Habitat House. It houses many animal species gathered for children in a living laboratory. Students assume a wide range of animal-care tasks. Lunch periods find my room a veritable beehive of activity. Like worker drones, children incessantly move about tending to their charges. A large magnetic chalkboard ruled off into a grid serves as the master scheduler. It lists a myriad of feeding details including animal names, cage numbers, food types, and amounts. Each animal has a small square magnet occupying the last square of the grid. It is coded with red on one side and green on the other. When a student scans the board for a task to complete, they immediately are directed to which jobs need to be done—they're green. Upon selection of a particular "green" job, the student must turn the magnet to red, signaling "Stop" to other children.

During an orientation session to Habitat House, a timid third grader patiently listened to my detailed procedures. When instructed, she approached the board and viewed her options. Her head rotated as she scanned the list. After an inordinate interval, she turned and looked at me. I labored toward her. She stated in a soft voice, "Mr. P, I need help. I want to feed the iguana but I can't." I bent down to inquire the nature of her problem. I gently probed, "Do you understand the board?" Her head bobbed in affirmation. Perplexed, I searched wider, "And, you know where the supplies are?" Again, she nodded. Her eyes, on level with mine, seemed tense and unsure. Remaining hunched to be close, I finally asked, "Well honey, what is it?"

She raised her hand, index finger extended and pointed to the chalk-board. Her arm was angled up and fixed on the iguana row. "It's too high, I can't reach to turn the magnet. Will you do it for me?" I momentarily froze, helpless, as I sensed my paralyzed arms hanging limply at my side. I seemed unable to help this young girl. She waited with an innocent stare that burned through me. I interpreted her body language as saying, "Well, are you going to help me or not?"

Whenever I faced the decision to continue to teach with severe disabilities, a haunting reality shadowed me. Will I recognize when the time comes that I should retire, when my limitations exceed my contributions?

Sixty-odd years ago, Lou Gehrig faced the same moment of truth. After a historic string of more than 2,000 games stretching thirteen years, Lou left baseball. "Leave at the top of your game" is a mantra spoken by all who are challenged by declining performance, and was certainly one I had wrestled. As I faced this young girl, I seemed on that cusp. I couldn't help her with the simplest request. I was hurting rather than helping. But this sweet, eager young child was about to teach me a lesson in life and about myself.

Intellectually, I always knew teaching was a magical interaction between the teacher and learner. John Dewey, the father of American education, captured it when he told us, "Learning is not a spectator sport." Yet emotionally, I was a prisoner of the need to "always know and to be in charge." ALS reshaped my world and forced me to reassess who and what I was. Now, this girl was doing the same thing.

I searched frantically for a resolution to her quandary. Gently, I asked her if she was aware of my muscle disease. She nervously smiled and whispered, "Yes."

"Well, hon, I can't help you. My arms are too weak. I can't raise them up that far," I confessed. Relieved at my own truthfulness, I nervously awaited her response. I anticipated her selection of a new animal, one that was literally more within her reach. Instead, she continued to just look at me. Her mind was focused; she wanted the iguana.

Suddenly, it came to me. "Hon, I can't solve your problem alone. But, if we work as a team, I think we can solve it together. Your arms are too short, my arms are too weak. If we help each other, we can do it."

I motioned to her to grasp my thin, limp arm. Quite reluctantly, recognizing the unorthodoxy of it all, she took my arm. "Great!" I exclaimed and encouraged her to push my arm up. Stretching on her toes and straining under the weight of my long arm, she inched my hand to the top of the chalkboard, a good six feet high. Her fingers pressed into the flesh of my upper arm and I heard a moan as she made a last effort. Hitting the magnet, my fingers managed to flip it to red. Spent, she let my arm go. It fell and thudded against my leg. Then, she left, content to do her job.

I stood there, the impact of what happened slowly sinking in. I realized I was no longer physically able. I understood I was no longer in charge of circumstance. I understood I couldn't be the solution. I also realized we needed to be a team, a true team united by common goals and purpose. I really learned our strength is in our collective abilities, not our individual weakness. After first hearing Dewey's words, it took me a while to finally get it— twenty-five years to be exact. Guess I'm a slow learner, but better late than never.

I continue to teach. My muscle deterioration advances. Each day brings a new challenge. It also brings an opportunity to learn and grow. ALS, rather than a death sentence, has become my master teacher.

CHAPTER 5

Maclean–Stevens Studios, Inc., 1998

Lessons Not in the Plan Book

Lynne M. Ellis

Mountain View Middle School
Goffstown, New Hampshire

We started that September knowing that it had the potential to be a year of extreme challenges. I was one of two teachers on a team composed of fifty-two eighth graders. On our roster was Eric, a boy diagnosed the previous spring with an inoperable brain tumor but who was undergoing experimental treatments. Shawna was part of us, too, a girl struggling with cystic fibrosis and desperately needing a double lung transplant. Also in our class was Ellen, a young lady in remission from leukemia but still receiving treatments. There was no way to have any clue where the year would take the fifty-four of us.

Believing that it was essential to start the year off with everyone having as much information as possible, we blocked off the full afternoon on the second day of school. Eric, Shawna, and Ellen sat quietly and factually told their stories, going into great detail. Eric showed students the shunt in his chest that pumped treatment into his body on a 24-hour basis. Ellen explained her leukemia and the pain of having spinal taps to check on the status of things. Shawna gave us the stark statistic of needing lungs before summer or moving close to the point of death. The students listened intently, asked sincere questions, and learned a great deal. They appreciated the honesty and respect that was shown and knew that we truly were together as a team. We left that afternoon with a deep sense of caring and commitment to each other. Little did we know that four days later my teaching partner's mother would pass away, drawing us together even more as the students supported her in that time of grieving.

Eric started the fall in a wheelchair, with almost no use of his left side.

He could not sit in a regular desk, and he needed to have an adult with him all day. After about a month of school he had to leave for a time because he was not able to maintain even his limited level of activity. We all lived in the uncertainty of what would happen to him. We were thrilled when in about five weeks he returned, slowly improving with tests showing the tumor had stopped growing and eventually started to shrink! And what a celebration for our team when Eric won the school spelling bee, moving on to the district level. On that day there were fifty-one students and two teachers who were as proud as any parent or family member could be.

One morning in February we were greeted by the news Shawna had been paged for her new lungs during the night. Students had the full range of emotions that day. They were thrilled at Shawna's new lease on life but were deeply scared about the complications that could be caused by a rejection of the new lungs. The day was filled with tears of joy and tears of fear from both the guys and the girls. We quickly put aside all curriculum plans and focused on the roller coaster of feelings that we all were trying to process. We talked, we listened, we wrote, we were quiet, we were loud— most important, we were together, and we walked through the first hours awaiting news. We went home with a plan to call every student at home if anything happened during the night. We knew that we would not want students walking into school unaware of anything traumatic. The plan was not needed, and day by day the news only got better as Shawna showed no signs of rejection. We even had her doctor come in and honestly answer students' questions, keeping them as fully informed as possible. Shawna came back to school two months later, and led us all through the changes her life now held. In May she participated in the annual cystic fibrosis walkathon, completing the route along with a team of about fifteen students and teachers. What an accomplishment!

In April, after having seen Eric and Shawna on their way to health, we were met with the tragic news one morning that one of our student's fathers had met an untimely death. Immediately our tight-knit family huddled together and comforted one another. Again tears were shed, questions were asked, and we tossed aside the lesson plans as we walked through one of life's toughest experiences.

June arrived, and we started the end of the year activities. Eric had regained use of his left side and was bouncing around almost like everyone else, now not needing to be on treatment twenty-four hours a day. Shawna was getting stronger and stronger as her body healed. Ellen was holding her own (though she did have a setback in the summer, which gave us all a scare). The student whose dad died had a long road ahead of her, but she was surrounded by people who loved and supported her. At the recognition ceremony on the last night of school, our class was the last to leave as each group was dismissed. One by one each student came by and hugged each teacher, some holding on a little longer than others. But they did not leave to go out with the other eighth graders for the refreshments. They gathered in the front of the gym, waiting for all of us to be together. We took more pictures, shared more laughter, tears, and hugs. No one wanted to break apart what had been so beautifully created over the year.

Personally, as the summer break started, I was drained—physically, emotionally, and mentally—from the roller coaster of emotions we went through together. But I had become a better person, which in turn leaves me a better teacher. For that I am thankful.

CHAPTER 6

Tim Lanterman

The Lifetime Achievement Award

Carla Woyak

Phoenix Children's Hospital
Phoenix, Arizona

wo years ago, I received the most precious gift a student could ever give a teacher. Eleven-year-old Leslie and I met at Phoenix Children's Hospital. She was there as a patient with cystic fibrosis. I was there as her teacher.

Leslie was full of life, emitting an energy that was contagious. She could bring a smile to your face even on your worst day. Her eyes held a sparkle that let you know that she had a purpose in everything she did. She was courageous, witty, and wanted to try everything life had to offer.

We called ourselves "soul sisters," and I truly believed we were. It started with our discovery that our birthdays were six days apart, making us both Leos, the "coolest" sign in the zodiac. We both loved the ocean and dolphins and the color purple. We both loved to sing to country music and dance around her hospital room.

The days I knew that Leslie was in the hospital were my favorite days to go to work. I would get up in the morning and plan what we would do that day on my drive in. Leslie loved to write, and she loved to do science experiments. More than that she loved to socialize with the other kids in the room. "What are you here for?" she would ask. "Who is your favorite nurse?" "Isn't the food totally gross here?" I would say to her, "Leslie, you need to focus on your work so everyone else can focus on theirs." She would look up at me with her award-winning smile and say, "I know, I know." One time, as she was sitting at the table wearing an oxygen tube to her nose, the tubing hooked to the wall across from the table, she responded to my usual statement by standing up and swinging the tubing like a boa around her neck.

She then began doing the moonwalk backward, away from me, laughing and singing a catchy jig: "can't catch me . . . la da da da la la da can't catch me . . . ." I just cracked up laughing.

Leslie and I also shared a love for Dr. Seuss. Once she happened to be in the hospital when we were celebrating Dr. Seuss's birthday. One of our activities involved the kids singing a newly made school song to the staff at the hospital. As I was setting up in the morning, Leslie walked up to me, pulling her oxygen tank behind her. She said, "Carla, I have always wanted to be a cheerleader and because of my stupid illness I will never get to be one. Do you think that I could be a cheerleader today for our celebration, just for our school song?" "Of course!" I answered. "Let me go find you your pompoms." I raced away, praying that I would have something in my closet that would resemble a pompom. My prayers were answered. I reached inside my closet and brought out two of the most obnoxious orange pompoms that have ever been seen. They were perfect! As I walked back to the hallway where I had put up the words to our song, I saw Leslie there reading the words and practicing her cheer movements. When I handed her the orange pompoms she let out a squeal of joy and starting shaking away. She told me she was going to take off her oxygen for the "real" performance. I ran to get my camera. Needless to say, that was the best school song I have ever witnessed.

That same hospital stay, Leslie had a science project due for her school's science fair. "How unfair!" she screamed. "I always miss out on everything because of my stupid disease." I said to her, "You don't have to miss out on anything, Leslie. We'll do your experiment here." At first she was skeptical, not knowing how we'd get the materials (her experiment was baking four batches of chocolate chip cookies leaving out different ingredients in each batch) and how we'd fit in the time between her medical treatments. After a few days of calls and gathering of materials, we were ready to start. I had reserved the adult therapy kitchen in the building next door, gained the doctors' permission, and rearranged her therapy and medicines. The nurses laughed at us as they saw me pushing Leslie in a wheelchair, oxygen tank strapped on the back, IV pole hooked up to one arm, and a cart filled with bowls, spoons, pans, and ingredients trailing behind us. Three hours later, after baking the four batches of cookies and taking a roll of silly pictures, we were done with step 1 of her experiment. Next, it was the taste test by the doctors and staff. But before she could write up the results, Leslie started to get sicker and wasn't able to leave her bed. Her goal was to finish this science project by the deadline. I came to her room daily wheeling a computer bedside so that I could type up her results and lay them out on a board for display. I remember having to stand on the end of her bed holding the board at an angle so that she could critique the layout of her papers while she lay on her back with tubes hanging out of her chest. Talk about perseverance. But, her hard work paid off. She ended up with a blue ribbon at her school's fair.

One month turned into the next, and I began to get the feeling that Leslie wasn't going to ever leave the hospital. Because of my special bond with Leslie, her parents had asked that I sit in on all of the meetings to discuss lung transplants and any other medical issues. I knew there would be a time when Leslie would have to spend what little energy she had on breathing and not be able to talk, so I started teaching her sign language. I told her this way we could still communicate and she wouldn't have to spend energy talking. I spent each day sitting by her side on her bed, teaching her the alphabet and various simple signs. But Leslie was becoming so tired. Her body was beginning to give up.

One day, as I was spending time in her room she said to me, "Carla, my mom and I have the best present for you but I can't tell you what it is." I said, "Leslie, you don't need to give me a present." She said, "No, this is better than a present, but I can't tell you what it is yet." Didn't she know that she was the best present I could ever get and that her mother gave me that gift by allowing me to become a part of their lives?

It was only a few days later, a Friday to be exact, that I was sitting on Leslie's bed face to face with her. I was telling her that I was going to be coming to the hospital on Saturday (which was not normally a day I worked) to help with a tour. I said that I was excited because that meant that I got to see her one extra day that week. We did a few signs, and then we sat in silence face to face for a very long time. I felt as though she was contemplating something quite serious, but I couldn't ask her what it was. I knew but I didn't want to know. She put her arm around me and let out a sigh as I bent down to kiss her cheek good-bye. I told her that I would come see her tomorrow, and I gave her a wink as I walked out the door.

That was the last time I saw Leslie awake. The next morning as I arrived to work I was told that Leslie was in the Intensive Care Unit and that she didn't have much time. I waited with her family, friends, and staff as she struggled to fight the illness that was taking her life. I was given the privilege of spending some time with her as she laid in her deep sleep. I whispered in her ear, letting her know how much she was loved by me and by all those around her. As tears streamed down my face, I witnessed the moment her last breath left her body. The fight was over. She could now run, cheer, jump, and do all of the things she always wanted to do but never could. How lucky the heavenly angels were to get her.

A few months later, I received a letter in the mail stating that I had been nominated for the Disney American Teacher Awards. A student had nominated me—Leslie. The nomination was her "surprise." What a bittersweet gift to receive. I cried tears of joy, for I had been blessed with knowing her. I cried tears of sorrow, as I couldn't thank her for my gift. I cried tears of anger, that such a dear young life had been taken away so soon.

I became one of the finalists in the awards, and I had the privilege to travel to Los Angeles for the celebration. After entering the hotel, I heard a song. It was Leslie's and my favorite song to sing in her hospital room. I like to think that was her way of saying hello. I like to think it was my chance to say "Thank you." The gift she had given me goes beyond her "surprise." That was just the beginning. The true gift is the realization that I had not been the teacher, but the one who had been taught. Thank you, Leslie. I will treasure this gift forever.

CHAPTER 7

Thos Mann

P.E.A.C.E.

Joanna Gallagher

Lyle Egan High School
Chino, California

As soon as I announced the offer—I had been offered a position to teach at Fred C. Nelles School for Boys, part of the California Youth Authority—the criticism began. Friends and family cried that I was wasting my time teaching teenagers in prison. After all, they were already failures; they were in jail! And was I thinking about my own safety, teaching high school English to drug-addicted, jailed gang members—these were murderers and rapists. Not to mention the fact that, according to CYA's policies, all students must attend school every day, all year. That would leave me with no summers off, no Christmas vacation, and an eight-hour workday, twelve months a year. I took the job, immediately.

Three months into it, I met Jesse. Like most of my students, Jesse had not attended school on a regular basis since sixth grade. When he did attend, by his own admission, he was high. He had been incarcerated at the age of fourteen for assault with a deadly weapon.

Jesse belonged to the Clover Street gang and carried with him the moniker of Lil Lion. He was small for his fifteen years, with the eyes of an old man and a number of learning disabilities. He wanted to earn his G.E.D. and become a sports writer for the *Los Angeles Times*. I spent hours working with him on Language Arts skills. I tutored him every chance we had. But we weren't getting very far. Jesse could not get his mind around memorizing the eight parts of speech and could not write a complete sentence without several glaring mistakes.

Then I created a mnemonic device: Not All Vatos (a Vato is a respected Latino) Are Pressure Cases In Prison. Taken in order, the first letter of each word in this sentence became his prompt to remember the parts of speech: N = Noun, Λ = Adjective, V = Verb, A = Adverb, P = Pronoun, C = Conjunction, I = Interjection, and P = Preposition. Together we also developed strategies so he could distinguish common and proper nouns. Eventually, Jesse not only knew the parts of speech, he knew their varied uses and applications.

In less than a year, Jesse did earn his G.E.D. and was paroled shortly after his sixteenth birthday. Several months later, one of his "homeboys" came to me with the news that Jesse had been murdered by a rival gang member as the result of a drive-by shooting. I locked myself in my classroom and sobbed. My tears were not for all my time and energy that now seem wasted, but for Jesse. For Jesse, who now would never have an opportunity to earn his dreams; for Jesse, whose smile when I handed him his G.E.D. results meant more to me than any awards or recognition I will ever receive.

Then I learned that he had not been murdered! His homeboy had been misinformed. I was overjoyed! About sixteen months later, I received a handwritten letter from Jesse. In it he told of enrolling himself in a journalism class and of the impending birth of his child. What I had learned about myself from that experience was how much I believed in the worth of each individual. The face of that small boy, with the courage of a lion and an ultimate belief in his own ability to change and grow, still appears in front of me whenever I become discouraged. It is Jesse's face that I see whenever I need to remind myself that the work that I do is important.

In the letter Jesse sent me, he ended it with a mnemonic device he created for me: P.E.A.C.E.: Please Educate And Care Eternally.

Thanks, Jesse, I will. I am a teacher.

CHAPTER 8

Sylvia Saunders

I Think I Can

Marilyn Lance

West Sand Lake Elementary
West Sand Lake, New York

At the time, I was a veteran teacher of about fifteen years and thought I knew a lot about teaching. After all, fifteen years is a long time in a career, and that benchmark might make one think she might be an "expert." I was accustomed to having children in my second grade classes with both academic difficulties and behavioral issues, so I felt I was well educated about children in need. Plus, my track record with children in need of intervention was fairly good.

Late in the spring of the year, my administrator informed me that the following fall I would have a child in my room named Courtney, who would have much difficulty learning anything but the simplest tasks. I was to do the best I could. She was to be in my class because there was not a slot for her in the more suitable out-of-the-district "special learning classroom" where she could acquire life skills. This better placement would have to wait until the following year.

That fall, school began again, and Courtney arrived. There she was, almost as tall as I was, with a heavy round tummy and thick, bowl-cut dark hair. Her knee-length dress was much too tight for her stout body, and the heavy black shoes she wore looked more like work boots than a child's comfortable play shoes. Her sweet round face had a wide smile that showed her crooked teeth sprouting out in every direction as she proclaimed, "Here I am, teacher!"

Before many days passed, I discovered there was so much more to Courtney than just a child with academic difficulties. Underneath Courtney's outwardly disheveled and awkward appearance, there was a kind, sensitive soul who expected nothing from others except gentleness in return.

As I watched Courtney day after day, I wondered what I could teach her that would be of value. What life skills would be useful to her? How could I make sure that I didn't waste a year of this child's life? I had many questions but few answers. As time passed, I discovered Courtney had some surprises in store for me. One of her great joys was to clean and organize. She would straighten up books on the classroom shelves, dust anything that was a flat surface, and keep the tables sparkling clean by washing them at least once a day. Courtney even adopted my desk as part of her mission for our room to be spotless. I would find my papers returned to my desk in neat, organized piles, all the pens and pencils I constantly left lying around in the correct containers, and the paper clips, rubber bands, and other miscellaneous items all carefully organized. When I couldn't find something, I knew a few questions to Courtney would reveal where she had put something. There were times when I really didn't want Courtney to find new locations for my books and manuals. I would patiently wait a few days and then quietly move items back to their original homes, only to find that Courtney would notice, chide me for "forgetting" where things went, and promptly put the items back in her selected spot.

Life with Courtney was never dull. Most of the other students were accepting of her, but had little to do with her. They didn't tease her or make fun of her; they just knew she was part of our room but "different." The one exception to this was Jimmy, a curly- and red-haired, impish, bright young man of seven who took great delight in making Courtney the target of his particular style of "pestering." While Jimmy wasn't a mean or malicious child, he certainly was mischievous, and he quickly discovered Courtney was easy prey. After Jimmy would play one of his tricks on Courtney, I would find Courtney hiding somewhere in the room or just sitting by herself with her head down. I'd redirect her, then head straight to Jimmy to try some one-on-one counseling about being kind to others and respectful of feelings. Neither my words, nor those of his parents, ever seemed to have any impact. The "pestering" continued, and Courtney didn't seem able to stand up for herself when incidents occurred. I began to notice Courtney's smile wasn't as quick when children approached her, and she would cautiously avoid any close proximity with Jimmy.

We had a tiny, windowless bathroom in our room with the light switch on the wall outside of the door. One day I noticed Jimmy standing by the bathroom waiting to enter. He had his back leaning up against the wall and was fidgeting as he stood there. Suddenly the bathroom door was flung open and out came Courtney. Jimmy had known she was in there and had purposely turned the light off. Courtney, red-faced, was glaring at him with fire and tears in her eyes, both angry and frightened. Jimmy smiled smugly and walked away. What was I going to do now? This was beyond anything that should be tolerated. I went home that evening wondering what my next steps would be. It wasn't long before the opportunity came in an unexpected way. I watched one afternoon as Jimmy went into the bathroom. What I did next was a surprise, even to me. I don't permit children to purposely be unkind to one another, but this was my exception. I motioned for Courtney to turn off the light on Jimmy. She stared at me with wide eyes as if to say "But I can't do that." With some quick encouragement, Courtney flipped the switch. It had taken all her courage but there she stood, filling up the entire opening as the door flew open. Jimmy had fire in his eyes. Courtney didn't move. Then, with her gaze firmly on him, she extended her hand with the simple words, "We're friends." It seemed forever before Jimmy put his hand out in return. "Okay," he said with a nod. Courtney moved aside and the two of them walked together back to their desks.

From that moment on, Courtney was different. She had dared to step outside of her safe "cleaning" box and had taken the first real steps toward believing in herself. She was still Courtney—kind, gentle, and trusting—but one also got the sense that she now had feelings of pride and self-worth. And so began Courtney's climb into the academic world as well. Despite the warnings about her abilities, Courtney began to learn.

First she learned to read simple words and moved right into easy books. She also began to understand basic math concepts—counting money was her favorite! But this is not just Courtney's story. While Courtney was certainly the protagonist, she was also the catalyst for growth and learning for both Jimmy and me. Jimmy was still Jimmy. But in many ways, Jimmy was "less" Jimmy. As for me, Courtney started me down the road toward always believing that children can achieve anything. The first step is making sure they believe it and never allowing them to think, "I can't."

CHAPTER 9

The Ripple Effect

Michelle Raiford Weeks

Tennille Elementary School
Tennille, Georgia

R ecently a friend called to tell me she was quitting her job at the end of May, to go back to school to pursue a teaching certificate. Needing encouragement and support, she wanted me to tell her why I teach. I told her the following stories.

Just before I entered the third grade, my family and I moved to a different state. On the day of open house when we were registering, the principal took us to my class. After I was introduced to the teacher, she told the principal that she didn't have room for any more students. Another teacher happened to be walking by and heard the comment. He told the principal that he would be more than happy to have me in his class. It was at that exact moment that I became infatuated with Bobby Crabtree. My parents and I were hurt by the comment of the other teacher, but the hurt was quickly healed by Mr. Crabtree's kindness. He was a loving teacher. His classroom was very structured, and his expectations were both high and clear. He made learning fun. I have many fond memories of his class. Some of those memories include each student getting a stuffed animal for learning their multiplication facts, going to the circus, visiting the Appalachian Museum, going on an overnight camping trip, and catching the bouquet at his wedding (yes, I was in the third grade at the time). I have often thought about Mr. Crabtree and my experiences in his room. He touched both my heart and my mind by teaching me more than academics. He taught me how rewarding a relationship between a student and teacher could be.

As a special education teacher, I am constantly amazed by my students' triumphs. They keep me focused on why I am an educator. One student who is especially dear to my heart has had a rough year. Since birth, he has lived with his grandparents. Last spring both of his grandparents were diagnosed with cancer. His grandfather died in December; his grandmother died on Valentine's Day two months later. The next day this student was at school. That worried me. My initial feeling was that he needed to be around his family. As the day progressed, I realized he *was* around family. When I told him how proud I was of him for coming to school, he commented that he was there because his grandmother would want him to be at school. I went to both funerals and sent him sympathy cards both times. I worried about who was going to take care of him. He spoke to me about the cards the day after his grandmother's funeral. Then he told me he had something else to say. When I asked him what, he responded, "I just had to thank you for caring about me so much." He did not know it, but he was taking care of me. His amazing strength and security decreased my worries.

I have a very clear memory of someone asking me when I was a child what I wanted to be when I grew up. I remember naming several possibilities and concluding the conversation by asserting I would "never be a teacher!" Once I said "never," the harder I tried to stay true to my vow and the harder I was pulled into the field. I am proud that I am a teacher. I am also thankful for all of the teachers I have had in each of my educational endeavors. They helped give me the confidence to reach out to students' hearts and minds. Without Mr. Crabtree's genuine love at a time when I was out of place and unwanted, I might not have ever learned how to care for a grieving student. Everyone should be so blessed.

CHAPTER 10

Alex Kamen

A Place caLLed Home

Kim Kamen

The Enterprise Foundation/AmeriCorps
Dallas, Texas

A s I entered into my first classroom that first day, I quickly realized that all the theories in the world hadn't prepared me for the twenty-two energetic pre-teens who wanted to be anywhere but there. Despite a rocky start (and a couple of frantic phone calls to my parents back East), I was determined to stay and make a difference in my students' lives.

One of the most surprising things I learned as I embarked upon my teaching career is that a significant number of the students who enrolled at a particular school would transfer out within several months. Their families would move two or even three times during the school year. The reason for this almost nomadic life was "apartment hopping"—the practice of taking advantage of "move-in specials" for low-rent apartments, which would promise free or reduced rent in return for three- to six-month leases. No wonder so many students were so far behind academically—they were constantly trying to catch up in new classrooms.

One morning, as I was taking roll, I noticed that one of my students, Lucila, looked extremely tired, and her clothes appeared disheveled. This had been the second day she seemed out of sorts. While many students had that glazed-over look first thing in the morning, Lucila was not one of them. Typically, she was the class clown and relished in gaining her classmate's attention, no matter what time of the day it was.

Later in the morning, I knelt by Lucila's desk and asked if everything was okay. She looked at me, smiled, and explained that her cousin had a baby the night before, and she was at the hospital very late. I had every reason to believe her. I knew Lucila's family fairly well and was aware she had a sixteen-year-old cousin who was pregnant.

I asked Lucila to convey my message of congratulations, to get some sleep that night, and went on with the day. However, the next morning, when Lucila did not come to school, I began to have my suspicions. She was out of school for the following two days. When the school could not reach her home to verify her absence, I knew something was wrong.

Although Lucila grew up in a single-parent household, her mother put a lot of effort into raising her children. Because Lucila's academic performance needed improvement, I had already met with her mother on several occasions. Whenever Lucila was absent in the past, her mother didn't wait for the school to call, she usually phoned in before school started and left a message for the secretary.

After Lucila's absence on the third day, I asked the school counselor to accompany me on a home visit. We made numerous attempts to call Lucila's home, to no avail. When we arrived at their run-down apartment, I peered into their curtain-less living room and was shocked to see it mostly empty. It looked like they left in a hurry; several boxes still remained in the living room. After conferring with the management office, we learned what we most feared—that Lucila's family had moved out unexpectedly the week before and didn't leave any forwarding information.

I returned to my classroom the next day with a heavy heart. I was frustrated that Lucila was whisked away so quickly—and concerned for her well-being. Did the family catch another "move-in special" or were they in some sort of trouble? The other students had begun asking about her whereabouts, and I didn't have the energy to come up with a creative answer when they asked that day, so I simply told them the truth.

What ensued was a conversation I'll never forget. We abandoned my lesson plans for the day, as we began to discuss such serious topics as the need for stability in our lives, the value of education, the challenges facing low-income people, and what it means to "make it" in America today.

Several students shared that their families "apartment hop" at least once a year, if not more frequently, and that they were tired of constantly moving around. Juan said, "Everyone in our family has a big box with our names on it. We keep most of our clothes in that box because it's a lot easier to pack that way. It's fun because we can decorate our box however we want, but I wish we had a real place to put our clothes away."

When I asked why they wanted to stay in one place, most of my students responded that they wanted to feel like they were in a house. This sparked an interesting discussion—why did it seem like most white people lived in houses, while most minorities did not?

Francisco explained that he was angry that his family had owned a home and land in Mexico, but when they moved to the United States, they suddenly had a lot less. Some students quickly agreed, while others pointed out that life in the countryside in Mexico was not as good as it was in the United States. They echoed their parents' sentiments when they said that they would have many more opportunities in America.

Naturally, this led to a heated debate: Do they have more opportunities in America? While most felt that indeed they do, a couple of students claimed that life in America was more difficult. In the Hispanic culture, youth were often expected to bide their time in public school until they were able to enter the workforce and help support the rest of their family. All too often, graduating from high school was reserved for the "lucky ones." At fifteen or sixteen, these young people had no choice but to take labor-intensive positions and never have the opportunity to think about further career opportunities.

One precocious student commented that his family, and so many others just like them, simply needed a permanent place to call home, a job they enjoyed, and hope for the future. All of us present couldn't have agreed with him more. It was a teachable moment for all involved.

CHAPTER 11

Cindi Butler, 2000

whatever it takes

Kelley Bowles Albaugh

Fruita Monument High School
Fruita, Colorado

have multiple sclerosis (MS). While it does not define me as a teacher or as a person, it is and will remain a constant fixture in my life, rearing its ugly head at the most unpredictable and inopportune moments.

I cannot talk about teachable moments without including MS, as it is forever a part of my life and my career. It has changed me as a person, giving me an empathy I never thought my perfect and emotionally spoiled upbringing would allow me to possess. I share information about my disease with students, and anyone who says kids "ain't like they used to be" has never seen my kids. They behave like perfect angels on days I don't feel well, and they treat me with a healthy curiosity and unbelievable respect on the days I do. My informative speech in speech class is about MS, and I have spoken in several science classes as well. A few students of mine are dealing with recently diagnosed family members, and I love to help them through their initial fear and anger. I think the fact that I talk about it instead of hiding it or always putting on a brave face allows them to experience compassion they might not have been aware they had.

As I have weak motor skills and cannot write well, students in my writing classes turn in cassette tapes with their essays, so I can hear and verbally grade their papers.

One of my most memorable students was Noah. Noah was a freshman in Lake Tahoe, California, during my first year of teaching. He was small and skinny and had very blonde hair that reached to his shoulders and stuck out of a baseball cap that was always pulled clear down to his nose. He wore bell-bottomed jeans that were way too long, so he dragged them along behind him in the dirt; they were his signature. One of my requirements for core English classes is outside reading, anywhere from 300 to 800 pages of books of the students' choosing. I let them pick for themselves because, let's face it, students often feel that the required reading for English is less than thrilling. Because my father owns a bookstore and has always brought home books as fast as I could inhale them, my theory is, "If you don't like reading, you just haven't found the right books yet!"

I shared this theory with Noah's class, and he confided to me that he had never actually finished a whole book. We talked for a while about his interests (snowboarding, girls, animals) and why he didn't like to read—books went too slow, books were boring, he could never get into them. I gave him a book by Dean Koontz called *The Watcher,* a thriller that involved a boy and his dog. He brought it back a week later; I was disappointed that this one hadn't worked. "That's not it," he said. "I'm finished. Give me another!" That year he read three Koontz novels, way in excess of the 500 pages I had assigned his class. I went back to Tahoe during Noah's senior year and discovered he had read something like twenty-five Dean Koontz novels and was looking for other thrillers to read.

Nobody would call Dean Koontz classic literature, but any reading is good reading, and I'd like to call writers like Koontz and Rowling the "gateway" books that lead to stronger and harder reading. I share my theory with all my English classes, and I have had one or two kids every semester say, "I don't like reading, so I must not have found the right books yet. Will you help me?" I have a library of my own in my classroom—books from my dad's store—ranging from thrillers to sci-fi to teen novels. I have yet to find a kid who wouldn't try to find the right books with me.

I've come to learn something about teachable moments. They come, well, not every moment, but certainly every day. And they travel both ways.

CHAPTER 12

Lifetouch, 1999

Heart Knowledge

Trish Culpepper

Vernal Junior High
Vernal, Utah

A junior high school is always entertaining. "A soap opera" comes closest to describing the events at any given hour. What determines the script for today depends on how fast you thought on your feet the previous day. You must be ever on guard, checking students for cryptic signs of impending needs. As a teacher, my job is to teach the masses while reaching out to the hurt, lost, or misdirected child. The quiet student with tragic eyes could just be a broken heart from an adolescent admiration or someone with serious suicidal tendencies. The athletic student body president with popularity dripping from his brow could have flawed leadership qualities that need redirection and training. The average student who dreams of better days ahead may need guidance to reach her full potential. The potentially most needy is usually the troublemaker, the person with "failure" stamped like a UPC symbol all over his face.

A troublemaker in the form of Jason came to my class like an unwanted blemish just before the big prom. He was another addition to an already difficult situation. The room was small and L-shaped. Desks were jammed into the room with little thought of comfort or educational disadvantages. This group consisted of mostly male low achievers at a second-grade reading level with sailor vocabularies and a "Test me if you dare" look written on every face. I was just beginning to make progress when Jason arrived. Immediately the power struggle began between us. We were sizing up each other when I discovered his Achilles heel. We had just begun reading as a group when I met his eyes. His fear telegraphed across the small room. I knew instantly that he could not read before his peers. Quietly, I circulated, and as I passed him, mouthed, "I will not embarrass you. Trust me." He seemed to relax. I timed the reading so he had a very short and easy read. He passed with flying colors.

In that moment, Jason realized my class would be different. He would have a place in class but not a disproportionate place. Jason could still impress his friends, but he would do it outside my room. Once inside that small space, Jason was one of many students, and he teamed to share the attention with his classmates. What did he win by trusting a teacher? He won his self-esteem. What did I win? I won the war of ultimate leadership and gained an ally for my class. He taught me, once again, that human kindness usually wins over negativity. He taught me that heart-knowledge usually triumphs over head-knowledge. He taught me to come back and try again another day.

An American to Admire

Lotte Repp Casillas

W. T. White High School
Dallas, Texas

J anuary marks the beginning of the second semester. My policy is, by this time, to not allow any new students or transfers to my Advanced Placement United States History course because I have such large classes. However, when I returned this particular January to meet my first period class, there was one new boy seated at the back of the room.

Khoi was a small and very timid boy who wore large glasses with thick lenses. A recent immigrant from Vietnam, his language skills were limited and he appeared nervous. He told me he was transferring from another Dallas high school to W. T. White High School because he wanted a better education. I struggled to understand his broken English. I warned him that my history class was very rigorous. He looked at me and very seriously said he knew. How could I turn away someone who wanted so earnestly to learn?

Khoi amazed me. He was always the first student to my class. No matter how early I arrived, Khoi was waiting for me. He would immediately begin working, whether reading or doing his written assignments. His Vietnamese-English dictionary was always on his desk. We would sometimes discuss key concepts, or he would ask me to read his essays to see if he was on the right track. He did just fine—not only a success in history, but in all of his classes.

The next September I did not have Khoi in class, but I ran into him in the hall. He had grown several inches over the summer. He replaced his glasses with contacts and his timidity with a happy confidence. I was amazed by Khoi's mastery of the English language in nine short months.

Khoi's academic achievements resulted in his selection as a candidate for the National Honor Society. As a sponsor for the group, I made sure Khoi knew to pick up an application. I wanted to make sure Khoi was recognized for his achievements.

A few days later I was alone in my classroom, and the door opened with a dejected Khoi at the door. "Mrs. Repp, I am so sad. I cannot be in the National Honor Society," said Khoi. He flipped through the pages of the application and noted he had nothing to fill in for extracurricular activities, leadership positions, or other interests. Once again, the meek, scared Khoi reappeared.

I took the application form from Khoi and looked over the categories to complete. I smiled and said, "Khoi, you have more than achieved in these areas. Let me help you." Under each of the blank areas, I wrote the following: "I am a New American. I work hard daily to excel in my educational studies so that I will become a productive citizen."

After reading the entries, Khoi looked at me and his big smile had returned. I assured him that anyone who wanted to learn as much as he did was National Honor Society material.

Khoi was selected to be a member of the National Honor Society. This Christmas he came to my room and brought me a large holiday greeting card. I thanked him, and later I opened the envelope and read the note Khoi had written to me:

> Mrs. Repp,
> You are a great teacher.
> Khoi

Bobbie Mustapha, 2001

The Gift

Francis Mustapha

South Side High School
Ft. Wayne, Indiana

The morning I came to school and learned that one of my students had committed suicide was the saddest day of my life. Unfortunately, no matter how many students a teacher impacts, the one student we cannot reach stands out. I often wonder what would have happened if I had known that she was in such pain. To this day I cry thinking about her. She never learned what I had the gift of discovering—how precious life really is.

In Medina, the West African village where I was born, there was no school. No one in my village could read or write. Nevertheless, my attitude toward learning and the most basic foundation of my success came from this village. My amazing father, who founded the village and provided leadership for his brothers, cousins, wives, and many children, was a model of confidence and enthusiasm for trying new things. My mother, who bore nine children and saw only two of us survive childhood, denied herself even the simplest of luxuries to help with my school fees. She left me no doubt as to my worth or my responsibility to live up to her expectations.

When schools were started near my home, I was sent to a little school in the next town. Not only did I and the others study reading and math, we also carried sand and water and formed the mud bricks to build the school. The teachers had absolute power over us, even assigning us new names—a practice with which I disagree. But we knew that the teachers were the keys to our future, so we did anything they required. Grade school was followed by boarding school, where my friends and I were obsessed with studying every book we could get our hands on in the hope of gaining entrance to one of the two colleges in the country. I graduated first in my class with hope for a scholarship, but political practices gave all the spots to those with connections to the party in power. I was sent instead to teach math at a high school in the northern part of the country. So my first teaching experience came by default, and I had no formal training other than the memory of how my teachers had taught me. At that time I had no intention of making teaching my life's work. My mind was on finding a way to continue my learning. I must have shown some amount of aptitude, however, because an American biology teacher there showed his faith in my potential by buying me a plane ticket to Indiana and arranging admission to Marion College. Once in Marion, I was on my own.

Biology and soccer playing were the easy aspects of life at college. Cultural misunderstandings, racism, isolation from home, and financial problems were the hard parts. Fortunately for my survival, another biology teacher entered my life. Professor Margaret Hodson became to me a friend, supporter, and mentor. Upon the heartbreaking news of the death of my mother, she became my American mother. Taking her advice, I added teaching to my degrees in biology and botany.

After finishing both Master's and Specialist in Education degrees at Indiana University, I married and began a career teaching biology. For the next two years I taught in a suburban junior high school and a city junior high school. Then my wife and I took teaching positions in Liberia, West Africa, where I taught college and rural development courses and moonlighted at a local high school. My biology class of sixty-five was so crowded that students had to stand outside and look in the windows. After three years, we moved to my own country of Sierra Leone to teach in a rural teacher training college. My American wife and I both loved teaching there, but as the political, medical, and economic situations in my homeland deteriorated, we returned to Indiana where I had been offered a high school teaching job. I've been teaching there since 1983. My wife's and my life revolve around our schools and our two children. The African colleges in which we taught have been destroyed by war. However, back in my village, there is now an elementary school, and we have helped brothers, sisters, nieces, and nephews to go to the same boarding school I attended. Someday, we hope to go back to teach in Africa.

Through the years, my attitude toward American students has changed. At nineteen, I could only see that American students had everything. Now, I realize that many of them lack the support, the values, and the confidence that I was fortunate to have in such abundance. There are also gaps in their lives I am in a position to fill.

Maybe something good did come from my student's death. I took an hour in class that morning to tell my students what had happened and how we must go on despite the tragic death of our close friend. I told my students, "If any of you have a problem, do not let it overwhelm you that you try to take your life. Find someone—anyone—to talk to, and if you don't think you have anyone to talk to, my friends, come talk to me."

After school that day, one of my students came to my room and we talked. From then on, Karen came to me with all of her problems and I listened. Ultimately she graduated and chose to take biology in college and major in genetic engineering.

I still replay that last day in class with the student who killed herself. Could I have done something to make a difference? But Karen has helped me more than I could have ever helped her. She gave me the chance to create an opportunity for her to succeed, as my village and my teachers did for me. She let me know that although one life was lost, another was saved. I will always be a teacher.

Christopher Ryan, 2000

save the children

Robin Zeal

Muldown Elementary
Whitefish, Montana

Michael was a stocky, talkative first grader. He worked with me for an hour each day, with other first graders who were just beginning to learn to read. It was easy to imagine Michael in high school, a linebacker on the football team. It was equally easy to see him as an adult, enjoying a beer and good company down at the local bar and grill. He was an affable, lovable kind of a kid. He would do anything to please me, and I'd probably do the same for him.

It was a snowy Monday in early December. I was modeling how to make a "list" for my students. Christmas seems to be a good time to talk about lists, because Santa is so interested in them. I always try to make my lessons fun by exaggerating, and today's lesson was no different. My learning objectives for this lesson were twofold. First, I wanted my students to understand and be able to write a numerated list. Second, I wanted them to write several adjectives in order to increase their application of letter sounds and help them with reading. I rarely think about the words that I will write until I'm writing them, so as I stood before my eight eager beginning writers, I created the following list:

I want . . .

a big, shiny, blue car

a fancy, huge, red house

a brand-new color television set

a superfast yellow snowboard

a bright, sparkling diamond ring

My students followed my lead and wrote their own lists to Santa. Theirs were far more reasonable—they actually had a chance of receiving some of their requests. The day continued on with four more classes, four more lists, and before I knew it, I had gone home, done my "Mom" thing, gone to bed, and it was time to get up again. Ugh!

I arrived at school, walked through the cafeteria in order to get my "fix" of a few hugs on my way to my classroom, and got ready for the day. Suddenly, Michael burst through my door, beaming from ear to ear. He bellowed, "Ms. Zeal, I have a present for you. It's one of the things that you wrote on your list yesterday!" With that announcement, he held out a wad of pink facial tissue. I was secretly hoping for the car, as mine was on its last legs, but realized, right away that, if this was a car, it wouldn't be big enough to hold my family.

I carefully opened the crumpled pink bundle and was startled to see something sparkle. Michael's eyes were sparkling, too. Wrapped inside was a beautiful diamond ring. Of course, I admired it and thanked him profusely for his thoughtfulness. I knew, right away, that this was not a dime-store ring, so I cautiously asked him where he had found such a beautiful piece of jewelry. He explained that his dad had taken him shopping and that they had bought it just for me.

I have received some very lovely presents during my many years in the public school classroom, but nothing as expensive as this. I knew that his parents appreciated my efforts in teaching their son to read, but this was carrying things a bit far. I decided that this was one gift that I could not accept. During my lunch break, I called his father, wondering how Michael had come up with such a beautiful gift. I was not prepared to hear the answer to my query.

Michael's dad tearfully shared the details with me. During the past few months, Michael's parents had been having difficulties in their marriage. The previous weekend, his young mother had reached a point of no return and left the family for good, setting that diamond ring on the kitchen table on her way out the door. Apparently, Michael had found it and decided to give it to someone who wanted it. He had brought it to school without his father's knowledge.

As I listened to the pain in Michael's father's voice, I was stunned. I didn't have any idea what to say to this man or to his son, either. Eventually, I pulled myself back into my professional shoes, offered some advice about counseling for Michael, made arrangements to safely return the ring, and hung up the phone. I found Michael on the playground and brought him to my classroom so that I could explain why I was giving back his precious gift. I explained to him how special the ring was to his mom and dad. I explained how much his parents must have loved each other when they exchanged it as a symbol of their marriage. I explained how much his parents love him now. I explained how much I loved him, too. He smiled his robust smile, and, giving me a "humungous" hug, rushed back outside to play.

This event happened several years ago. Michael's parents have since divorced, and he is living the rubber-band life of millions of children, stretched between two parents and two homes. He continues to love life, offering his incessant smile and indomitable spirit to anyone who'll receive it. I will always treasure this story of Michael's special gift, because it is a poignant reminder of how much impact I have as a teacher. In the eyes of my students, I possess more prestige than any doctor, more clout than any lawyer, and a daunting power to help or hinder their growth as productive human beings. At times, I might even replace a missing mom.

Lens Art Studios, 2000

we teach–no matter what

Juley Harper

Delmar Middle School
Delmar, Delaware

W hy did I become a teacher? Never have I wanted to do anything else. Teaching is not only what I do, but who I am. I believe that the word *teacher* is the most revered word in the English language. It is synonymous with compassion and is symbolic of the many facets of our vocation, for teaching requires a passion for giving to others.

I had the opportunity of a lifetime; it was an opportunity to give to others beyond the four walls of my classroom. My husband was asked to fulfill a one-year mission in Bosnia with the United Nations on the International Police Task Force, and I felt compelled to go with him to see what I could do for the schoolchildren there. My husband went out three months early to find a place for us to live and to make sure it would be safe for me to come. My school granted me a year sabbatical, and I packed our home in boxes and set off for a war-torn country whose images I had only seen on television.

When I stepped out into a dim fog from the brightness of the airplane, I had only one thing on my mind—survival! This airport didn't have any windows. The stench of thick smoke smacked me in the face as the door to the airport was opened. There were no employees waiting to greet us. In their place were men dressed in disheveled uniforms that were much too big. Each man held a gun in one hand and a cigarette in the other. They glared at each of us as we passed. There was not a luggage claim area. As a matter of fact, I wasn't even sure I'd see my luggage again. I would later find out that many of the people on our flight did not. When I looked over at Dale through eyes that were running, half from the smoke and half from fear, he tried to comfort me by squeezing my hand and joking, "Welcome to the Sarajevo Airport." I realized then that my husband was right when he told me not to worry that I hadn't found the peach-and-gray carry-on that completed my set of luggage. He was right when he said it was okay if my clothes weren't starched and creased before we left. He was right when he said that the few extra minutes that I needed to paint my nails before we loaded the car to go to the airport were minutes wasted. These people had problems—big problems. The rose-shaped bomb holes under my feet, the shattered windows, the three light bulbs that hung from the ceiling by poorly covered electric wires, and the presence of international police were evidence of that. This was a war-torn country. The menial problems that I had before I landed in Bosnia-Herzegovina were irrelevant to these people.

I never felt such an overwhelming rush of sadness as I did that day, and the feeling would not leave me for the next year. The only smiles I saw were from the people of the other countries who were there to provide assistance to the survivors of the war between the Muslims, the Serbs, and the Croats. They smiled because they knew they could leave Bosnia once their mission was over. But those who lived and breathed the war knew that although the bombs were no longer flying through the air, the hardship felt between the people and the evidence of the war would be forever present.

We loaded the UN-issued Land Rover with our luggage and headed down the tired old roads to our home. As we traveled along the streets I saw devastation everywhere: burned-out buildings, people dressed in tattered clothing, hundreds of thousands of tombstones, broken-down cars, women covered from head to toe in black clothing, and filthy children playing with whatever makeshift toys they had created. The air was filled with the smells of defecation, urine, and rotting vegetables. Although there was no humidity, the atmosphere was thick with fog, and it was hard to breathe. I sat in utter amazement, trying to hold back my tears. Dale had learned to live and not be broken by the sights, but this was all new to me.

It took me a month to venture out on my own. I learned enough of the local language to get around. I learned to take the tram into the city of Sarajevo to meet Dale for lunch. I learned to shop for dinner at the local outdoor markets, and I even learned how to ignore the smells of the local people. I began to acquire a taste for the food and appreciate a different culture. I was proud of myself. Dale and I would travel into Sarajevo, a city of 300,000 people, and order a pizza and feel normal again. But when we walked the five miles back home because we didn't have a vehicle and the tram had stopped running for the night, we were reminded of the destruction. And when we arrived at our apartment, a small four-room bungalow above a Muslim family, only to find that we had no electricity or water, we had to remind each other why we were there. I knew I was there to be with Dale, but I felt that I wasn't contributing to the cause. That's why I began to tutor the child of our Muslim landlords.

Belina was fifteen and could speak three languages fluently, but she was having trouble with English and needed me to help her. In return, she would teach me the Bosnian language. At first we had a tough time trying to understand each other, and we relied heavily on the Bosnian-American dictionary. Soon we learned to understand each other and developed a friendship. I looked forward to her visits. I asked her to water our plants and watch our apartment when Dale and I traveled to London for my birthday. Upon our return, we discovered that Belina had stolen the perfume that Dale had given me for my birthday, had used my makeup, and had invited people over to watch a hockey game on our television. When I confronted Belina, she was defensive but eventually admitted to wrongdoing. Dale and I felt betrayed, but I made the decision to continue tutoring her in hope of teaching her a sense of morals. I saw Belina smile a lot over the next year as she became more comfortable with the English language and grew as a young lady as well. Belina showed me where the neighboring schools were, and I ventured out to observe the education that was being offered in Bosnia. I visited schools where sunlight was the only light. Seldom did students have books or pencils. I led a school-supply drive to help those teachers and students. That experience taught me the truth of what good teachers everywhere do. We teach no matter what the situation.

I discovered many things in Bosnia, all of which pertain to Americans having very good lives. We have many modern conveniences that Bosnians will never be able to afford. Running water and electricity are the bare necessities that they cannot depend on and we so often do not appreciate. I have not even mentioned grocery stores, televisions, movie theaters, and fast-food restaurants. Those places are scarce in Bosnia.

Americans have a sense of self-pride that people who have survived a war in which neighbors and family members killed each other will never have. We have manners. We do know that if we want something we may have to stand in line, and we know not to blow smoke in other's faces. We also know not to push others out of the way to get where we're going. We know how to smile and say "Hello" when others greet us.

Every morning as I get dressed for school I listen to the news reporters telling me about the terrible things that continue to happen in Bosnia and in other countries all over the world. I wish that my husband and I could dedicate our lives to traveling to these areas to help, but until then I will tell my students about it. These students are our future leaders, and if I can encourage just one student to want to give to others then I am making a difference.

Margie Simpson, 2000

The School of Life

Trish Hill

East Handley Elementary
Ft. Worth, Texas

t had been an amazing school year. I had been selected as outstanding teacher to represent my school for the 1998–1999 school year in our district. I had been blessed with a great class and a wonderful room mother. Together, we had made a beautiful class quilt in celebration of the Fort Worth Sesquicentennial. After the children completed twenty squares, my room mother added the sashing, and her seventy-nine-year-old grandmother quilted it by hand for us. At age fifty-two, I was a very busy, fulfilled teacher, feeling good about the memorable experiences I had shared with my class. Life was good and I was on top of the world.

Then, the bottom fell out. I had scheduled my annual mammogram, which was four months past due. I had felt a couple of lumps, but had put off making an appointment until after school was out for summer. I didn't want any inconveniences to get in the way of teaching. Besides, I had convinced myself they were just fibroids.

But I was wrong. The radiologist informed me they weren't fibroids, and that I needed to see a surgeon for a biopsy. Within three days of the test, I was in the hospital having a lumpectomy and lymph node dissection. Even though the cancer was only 1.6 cm, it had spread to surrounding tissue. Recommended follow-up treatment would include four rounds of chemotherapy and thirty-seven radiation treatments. I spent the next month recovering from the surgery and working to regain use of my left arm. As this whole nightmare unfolded, I kept thinking how fortunate I was that this had happened in the summer, so I wouldn't have to miss any school.

It never entered my mind that I couldn't be a patient and teacher at the same time. My oncologist had assured me up front that he had treated many teachers who came in for chemo on Friday and were back at work on Monday. Another teacher at my school had gone through it several years ago.

It didn't mean that I was taking my situation lightly. I knew women who had died of breast cancer. My son's math teacher had just died the year before, less than a year after her diagnosis. I was trying to be positive and confident, but I was frightened and worried. I was also angry that I had always tried to take good care of myself, and yet this little uninvited alien had invaded my body!

School started in early August. My first day back, I walked into the office to find a beautiful plant with a beanie baby attached to it. It was from my room mother from last year. She was a serious beanie baby collector. The card read, "This is 'Halo' the angel bear, to watch over you during your treatments." It had a special meaning because our school mascot was a bear.

I had purposely put off starting the chemotherapy as long as they would let me, so that I could get the school year started with my new class of first graders. I wanted to establish routines before I began the dreaded and much feared ordeal. I had no way of knowing how my body would respond to the treatments until I had actually started them. I wanted to maintain as much consistency with the children as possible. I even found a substitute who would be able to fill in for me each time I had to be out for a treatment.

I sent a letter home to the parents to let them know what I was about to begin and that they need not worry about their children's education being compromised. The day before my first chemo, I explained to the children that I had breast cancer, and I had surgery to remove it, but I would need to receive some strong medicine to kill any cancer that they had missed. Several children had relatives that had been through it and were eager to tell me how sick I would be and that my hair would fall out. I tried to prepare them for the day when I would walk in with a new hairdo.

Two weeks into the school year, armed with Halo and my John Tesh CDs, I had my first round of chemotherapy. I was back at school on Monday, but faded fast as the day wore on. My classroom is in a portable building, and we were still having temperatures in the hundreds. Every time I had to face the extreme heat, it would zap me. Two weeks after my first treatment, my oncologist put me in the hospital for four days over Labor Day weekend.

My white count was very low, and I was running a fever. All I could think about was getting the fever down so I could get out and go back to school.

I was very fortunate through all of this to have a supportive, loving husband and family, newfound survivor friends at church, and a wonderful, understanding principal, whose wife had been diagnosed with breast cancer three years earlier. I also worked with two of the best teachers (and friends) anywhere, who were always there to lighten my load on my worst days. I never could have gotten through it without everyone's prayers and acts of kindness.

But it was the love of the children that truly carried me through those rough times. I knew that when I got out of bed in the mornings, if I could put one foot in front of the other one, I needed to be at school. I seemed to do better during the week when I was busy with teaching, though exhausted, than on the weekends when I'd lie in bed feeling sorry for myself.

I felt like there were other angels besides Halo watching over me. I would go in every Friday for blood work, only to find that my white count was often dangerously low. I had been exposed to every germ imaginable, having been in the company of six- and seven-year-olds all week, but I never got sick. We teachers often laughed about my class not just learning how to read, write, and do math, but also learning how to cough and sneeze into the folds of their arms.

The most disappointing part of the chemotherapy was all the fun things I missed with my class—the Halloween Carnival, zoo trip, storybook character parade, and pie throw with our principal. I finally received my last round of chemo in November. I spent the next few weeks just trying to recover from the cumulative effects. Once my counts were back up, I started the long regimen of radiation.

Being a teacher, I'm always trying to take advantage of those teachable moments throughout the day. The day my radiation started I decided to make a pink paper chain numbered 1 through 37 and hang it from the ceiling of my classroom. We made a counting backward lesson out of it. My treatments were given once a day, five days a week for over seven weeks. I had a standing appointment every day after school at 4:15. Each morning when the children arrived, my helper for the day would tear off the bottom link, so we could watch the chain shrink. As it became shorter, they delighted at having to stand in a chair to reach the next link. It was an encouraging sign to them that this long, drawn-out process was about to come to an end.

Every year I purchase little, red apple Christmas tree ornaments and write the children's names, my name, and the year on them and give them as a Christmas gift. This year I also painted the pink ribbon symbol on them as a reminder of what we had all been through together.

I received my last beam on January 25, 2000. The next day happened to be the 100th day of school, so we had a radiation graduation/100th day of school celebration. We had treats and goodies, and a dear minister friend from church brought his guitar and sang songs with the children. It was a great day for all of us!

My hair had been growing since November, but wasn't a respectable length until April. I came out of the wig on Easter Sunday. The next week we had a Popsicle party in honor of my popping off the wig.

What did I learn from all this? That giving all I had to give to those children (some days more, some days less) kept me going and gave me the strength to face another day on the way to the end of this unexpected detour in my life journey. They never expected or demanded more than I could give on any given day. They were always sensitive to my energy level.

The best part of this teaching moment was that it was an extended one. In addition to the required academic strategies, I have always tried to model and teach life skills to my children. I hope they never have to use this one. But I hope the lessons we learned would give them the strength and courage to deal with and rise above whatever challenges they may face in the future.

supermodeL

Madonna Boclair Hanna

Bremerton High School
Bremerton, Washington

'm a fashion-show coordinator and discovered that a fashion show used correctly is an excellent way to raise self-esteem and improve confidence, grooming, and personal hygiene. Putting on a fashion show with disabled individuals is really no different from teaching able-bodied people. Having done it many times, I've found a few things to be true:

Some people catch on quicker than others do.

Some want stars on their dressing room doors!

Everyone is nervous before the show.

Everyone dresses at different speeds.

The student who taught me the most valuable lesson was a young man I'll call "Romeo." He was a seventeen-year-old blind young man who had never been involved in a fashion show. (In fact, I needed to explain what a fashion show was to all the special needs students.) Once this young man understood what was going to happen, he was thrilled to become a part of the excitement! He enjoyed the rehearsals, the fittings at the local department store, and the photo shoot set up by the local newspaper. I marveled at his unbridled enthusiasm. There were times when my students and I wondered if Romeo could actually see, because his level of participation and awareness was uncanny! Romeo had three changes of clothes (yes, three): a two-piece beige ethnic ensemble, a very colorful active-wear outfit, and a tuxedo. He allowed my fashion students to frantically change him into the assortment of outfits and rush him onto the stage, where I was waiting to describe his garments.

When the day of the show finally arrived, I led him across the stage, as he exclaimed, "I'm having fun!" Romeo even danced with me! I had taught him a short swing dance routine. He kept asking me, "Am I dancing, Mrs. Hanna, am I really dancing?"

After the show I met his mother. She hugged me and whispered into my ear, "I'm Romeo's mother. Thank you, thank you, thank you. My heart cannot comprehend all the joy that was involved with this fashion show."

I cried. I will never forget the pride and love that beamed from her face and the faces of the other parents.

To this day, I continue to coordinate fashion shows that feature people with disabilities. The style shows are a true celebration of life, learning, and the quest to find beauty in all of humankind.

Romeo, wherever you are now, I thank you for inspiring me with your overwhelming enthusiasm, profound zest for life, and incredible ability to express your joy!

"when it's worse, ms. mac,
it only gets better"

Horizons Academy
San Angelo, Texas

Our differences stood out from the start—Robbie was male and I female. He was seven. I was forty-seven. He started his life with a mother who took drugs while she was pregnant with him. He had a bottle placed into the bed with him that he could neither reach nor hold. He cried constantly, getting sleep only in spurts of twenty minutes. My mother, who breastfed me, was the original health food advocate. I was a happy baby who walked early, talked early, and was taught to read before entering school. When authorities removed Robbie from his birth mother's home at the age of three weeks, he was covered with sores and weighed only five pounds. Because he was about one year old before he sat up and three years old before he said his first words, he was diagnosed as being developmentally delayed and labeled a "high risk" infant.

At the beginning it was not our differences that strained our relationship, it was actually our similarities. Both of us had lived in a county in Texas that had the reputation of having one of the highest number of child abuse cases per capita. Both of us were stubborn, and both of us did not like "systems," especially those that control instead of serve.

I came from a long history of teachers and a good education was always a priority for my family. I had founded my own private school/learning lab with grand ideas of saving children who seem to fall through the cracks in the regular systems. Motivated by my own son's problems in school, I knew that there were many children like him, who, though they had above-average IQs, were not equipped to handle the demands of a system that did not recognize their potential.

My school had been in place for six years when Robbie walked through the door. My heart went out to him immediately; he was small for his age due to thyroid problems and he had a "lost puppy dog" look to his face with big sad eyes.

I have never turned down an application from a family with a child having a problem. I have viewed every child as having high potential. I have been willing to make concessions for children as long as the parent was actively pursuing answers to their own behavior or attention problems. My formal instruction concerning "crack babies" or "drug babies" was limited. I was willing to help any child with any learning style, but I was concerned that drug-exposed children often have an inability to recognize right from wrong or to show signs of empathy.

Robbie's problems created many others within the classroom. He would openly steal things and deny that he took them. Diagnosed as a child with oppositional authority disorder, he defied my guidance, my instructions, and my corrections on a daily basis. We often butted heads.

He, like other children of his circumstances, did not like to be touched. Hugs or a pat on the head were not well received. Positive reinforcement was hard. He was easily distracted by noise and he misinterpreted social cues, which often got him into conflicts with other students. His handwriting was illegible.

Understanding him would not be enough. I knew that his behavior would always be in question, and I knew that the "system" would not respect him because of this behavior. So I set out to make his academic achievements impressive enough to demand enough respect to provide him clout in the educational world.

When Robbie was exposed to my unconventional way of teaching math, which allowed him to create stories and perform puppet shows, he hugged me and told me that I was the best teacher ever. I thought I was over the hill in my attempts to reach Robbie.

Not so—some days were wonderful; others were more than trying. The experts who were helping with his behavioral problems and his growth problems were adjusting his medications. But they did not seem to have all the answers, and the changes were coming too slowly. His adoptive mother wore down and was hospitalized for a much-needed rest. I felt that I also was wearing down. Every step forward seemed to be lost in a step backward. I am not sure what kept me going. Maybe it was because I knew that if I couldn't help Robbie, the system would eventually eat him up. And like Robbie, I was stubborn.

It was a usual "Robbie" day at school when we turned the corner. Robbie was more than difficult on this day. He had been talking a lot lately about his brother, who had been, years before, sent to a special residential facility for emotionally disturbed children. Listening to other children talk about their families took its toll on Robbie. However, the unusual fact that influenced this day actually occurred several months before. My son was abused in the same county in which Robbie had been neglected and abused. I sent my son to live in another city with relatives. I was full of guilt over my failure to protect my son, angry at the indifferent systems, and longing to reconnect emotionally with my child.

On this day I had corrected Robbie more than twenty times and put him in time-out twice. I tried to reason. I tried praise. And like a broken record, I preached and reprimanded over and over. When he hurt another child, I had had it. Taking Robbie by the arm, I stepped into the hall. I got down on my knees and, looking at him eye to eye, I shook my finger and preached one more sermon. Robbie did not flinch, pout, or even smile, fueling my frustration because he not only showed no remorse, but only stubborn indifference.

I clinched my jaw, counted to three, and sat back on the floor. I threw up my hands and told Robbie that I was giving up. I had tried everything from loving hugs and rewards to tongue lashes. I was tired of it and I was giving up. His facial expression softened a little.

"Why?" I asked. "Why?" His fact contorted, and the tears that I thought would have come with remorse now came with sorrow. He hesitated as if he were revealing a secret. "I just miss my brother," he sobbed.

That was all I needed to hear. I fell apart sobbing, "I miss my son." Robbie reached for me and we hugged; we cried in each other's arms, consoling each other gently. My floodgates were larger than his were, and he continued to soothe me as I released my pent-up tears. "Don't worry, Ms. Mac," he stated, "when it is worse, it can only get better. I should know, I have had lots of worses."

Walking back into the classroom with red eyes and nose, I announced that Robbie had taught me something—that sometimes we act defiantly because we hurt so much and so deeply that we do nothing else. Then Robbie told the other students about his brother. The class responded in a supportive manner and began discussing their fears and even admitting to some of their ill-gotten behaviors. There were so many hugs given that I couldn't tell who needed them more—Robbie, the rest of the class, or me.

The courage needed by teachers to make a difference is not necessarily implementing bold curriculum ideas, taking controversial political stands, or even fighting irrational bureaucratic demands. The courage needed is simply to be willing to listen to and learn from your students ... even from a very young "failure to thrive" child.

CHAPTER 20

Ginny Twersky, 1997

In Loving Memory

Ruth Ritterband

Solomon Schechter Academy
Dallas, Texas

In February 1995, a student of mine, Seth Weinstein, a senior at the Solomon Schechter Day School of Essex and Union, boarded a plane with thirty-five of his classmates to spend three months in Israel on a special school program. The program is called NESHAMA, which is a Hebrew word that means "soul."

At least 75 percent of the senior class annually participates in this program. For Seth, however, it was truly a milestone. Just days before the start of his senior year, he fell ill, seriously ill. Within weeks, he and his family had learned that he was suffering from a brain tumor, which had been growing undetected for an extremely long time. He resolved to handle everything with the patience and determination and commitment that already marked his behavior. He came to school despite the fact that four or five times a week he traveled into New York City with his mother to Columbia Presbyterian Hospital for radiation treatments. When the NESHAMA applications were filed, his was among them. Not for a moment did I ever waiver in my resolve that he would attend. If he could do what he needed to do, we could do likewise. He proceeded through the necessary interviews, wrote the requisite essays, and made plans to attend with his classmates. When I, as head of school, hugged and kissed the kids good-bye at Newark Airport, I handed him his x-rays for the doctors in Israel and wished him well. He shyly thanked me for letting him go; it was hard to stop crying on my way home.

Seth made it reasonably well through most of the program, but his activity tapered off as his fatigue increased. He returned home with the group and graduated with them in June. He died six months later. His class and I met again in grief, at the synagogue. From there we drove to the cemetery; we all, as is our custom, turned a shovel of dirt into Seth's grave, his final resting place. The personal courage, the quiet strength, the beauty of Seth Weinstein's soul that endured such pain and such challenge—all of these qualities taught me new dimensions of the human condition.

Chuck Kenck, 2001

everyday miracles

Raschelle R. Freeman

(a.k.a. Dr. Pattern)

Robert E. Lee Elementary
East Wenatchee, Washington

Dedicated to Tommy...who taught a teacher a thing or two

After teaching in a self-contained classroom ranging from third to sixth grades, I was ready for a change. I had received some recognition for my mathematics and science instruction. It was time to dream beyond the walls of my classroom and reach out to more children and an incredible staff of teachers. After writing and receiving several grants, I was able to start a wonderful new program in my school entitled, "The SMART Museum." With approval from staff and the district, I became Dr. Pattern, and 450 children would come to my room every week. My job was to spark the curiosity of every first- though fifth-grade child and teach them how to think critically using science and math.

As I began to prepare during the summer, tiny whispers of fear entered my thoughts. How in the world was I going to set up this program? I wouldn't have my own twenty-eight unique students six hours a day for 180 days. I would be teaching other teachers' children. What had I gotten myself into? Furthermore, first graders would be coming to my room! I think this scared me most of all. Yes, I am a certified teacher, but there is a distinct delineation between intermediate teachers and primary teachers. I admired every primary teacher I encountered and considered them miracle workers. I was an intermediate-age teacher through and through. How does one engage a six-year-old in the art of learning? How does one engage *twenty-seven* six-year-olds in the art of learning all at the same time? However, none of these doubts stopped the school year from beginning, and soon I was in the thick of it.

Every day from 12:15 to 1:05, a class of first graders visited the SMART

Museum. My lesson plans for this fifty-minute period took me twice as long to prepare as all the other four grades put together. The youngsters entered the room with energy unsurpassed by a locomotive train coming downhill. I soon started taking deep breaths at 12:10 to prepare myself for the onslaught. After the students left, I felt like a small tornado had visited the room and was relieved as it went spinning down the hall to the first grade teacher.

My husband was in the habit of finding me tidbits for my room. He loved nature and looked upon it with a different lens than I did. One day he found a fallen bird's nest with a whole, small, white, speckled egg inside. He suggested I put it on display in the museum. I didn't think much of it, but I took it to school, and laid it on a shelf. Ho hum. I was too busy preparing complex science labs and challenging math problems to give it a second thought.

The next day, I entered a first grade classroom to do a lesson using small round plastic pieces to solve the math problems. At the end of the lesson, the children put the plastic pieces back in my tubs, and I began to wheel them away.

Before reaching my room, I heard a voice calling, "Mrs. Doctor, Mrs. Doctor!" I turned and there was little brown-eyed Tommy scooting down the hall to meet me. "Here's one of your circle pieces!" he exclaimed. I thanked him and sent him on his way, thankful it was now my prep time so I could be alone. I sat down at my desk hidden away behind bookshelves to complete some paperwork. Then I heard a little pitter-patter out in the museum and poked my head around a shelf. There was Tommy again. He held up another plastic circle, saying, "We found another one." I smiled and sent him on his way.

Not five minutes later I heard another pitter-patter. I again peeked around the shelf. Yep, it was Tommy. So proud and full of the responsibility his teacher had given him. Another missing plastic circle had been found! It didn't stop here. He returned two more times! On the fourth return I almost told him that if he found any more to just give them to his teacher and I would make sure I came and got them myself later on in the day. I am glad I didn't.

When I heard the pitter-patter for the fifth time, I was ready for him and held out my hand to receive the plastic circle. Our eyes connected, and he just stared at me. With my hand still extended palm up, I asked him for the piece. He mumbled that he didn't have another one. "Well then," I said, "how can I help you, Mr. Tommy?" By this time his eyes were as big as saucers. I followed his eyes over to my shelf where they landed upon the bird's nest.

He said, "I told my teacher I had found another piece so I could come back. I noticed you had a bird's nest there, and I really wanted to look at it."

Deciding to foster his curiosity and postponing a discussion on the importance of honesty for later, I led him over to the shelf. He noticed the little egg and asked if it was real. I told him as real as real can get. He continued to stare with inquisitive eyes and finally looked up at me and said, "Dr. Pattern, do you think you could check out some books on birds and have them in the museum? The next time I come I want to figure out what kind of bird laid that egg."

Isn't it the simple things? Six-year-olds are already curious and inquisitive people. Where does this go when we become adults? Suddenly I realized I did not have to spend long hours lesson-planning for these youngsters. I merely had to bring the small miracles around us that exist in a backyard, in a park, on the ground, and even in the refrigerator. Yes, it really is the simple things.

CHAPTER 22

John Boyen, 2001

seeing the potential

Jennifer Boyen

Braun Station Elementary
San Antonio, Texas

I f you ask most teachers to tell you the most memorable moment of their teaching careers, I guarantee you they can't. At least, I know I couldn't think of just one. I can think of many, perhaps even hundreds. Each school year is special in some way. Each student leaves a memory, whether good or bad. Sometimes, as a teacher, you remember that one student who was difficult. Or maybe it's that shining star—you know, the student who always put forth 100 percent, always behaved, almost seemed too good to be true. One of my most memorable moments in teaching came from a child who was both of these types of students.

Before I can share with you more about this student, I must give you some background about the school in which I taught at the time. Inner-city Houston is one tough area. The school was 98 percent minority students, 95 percent economically disadvantaged students, and yet the children were extremely successful. So successful in fact, they gained national recognition from people like Oprah Winfrey; even *20/20* did a story on this school. This was a Texas Exemplary School, a shining star amid poverty and crime. What was the secret? Hard work, ability grouping, direct teaching (better known as "drill and kill" to some), strict administration, and children who were told they would succeed. This was a place where some teachers would quit after only days or be fired after only months. I spent my first month crying at the end of every day. At the time, teacher turnaround was nearly 75 percent at the end of each school year, yet the children succeeded. Perhaps these children had an internal motivation that was so strong it conquered all obstacles.

My fourth grade class for this year consisted of twenty-four students, twenty-three African Americans and one Hispanic student. This group was called "the third group," ability-wise. This meant two classes worth of children were smarter and harder working than they were, and they knew this. Their goal was to get into a higher group. Johnny had been in the bottom group in first grade and had become a successful reader only in the third grade, which allowed him to move up to the third group, my class.

He had always been a behavior problem. Johnny often had more on his mind than reading. His grandmother was raising him; his father was in jail, his mother still trying to grow up. How could Johnny be expected to concentrate with that kind of family life? Well, this school expected that and more.

Johnny was not an exceptional case; almost every child in my class was in a similar situation. Yet daily, they were expected to work hard, so hard that they didn't even get recess. Lunchtime was silent, only reading allowed. There was no time to waste, but Johnny was a student who needed time to waste. This school was not the right environment for his personality and learning style. He was creative, artistic, and intelligent in a way that was not being fostered. Only the children in the top class, those considered "gifted," were allowed to learn in a variety of ways. I had to teach my class exactly the way the administration required. This way of teaching did not meet Johnny's needs, yet I could do nothing about that, at least not right away.

Johnny and I battled for the first few months. He could not sit in a chair. At a more prominent school, someone might have diagnosed him with ADD, but not here. No one had the time, money, or insurance to diagnose those kinds of problems. Johnny would often get so frustrated he would become disrespectful and refuse to work. Three times in the first month the assistant principal removed him from my room.

Slowly, as the year progressed, I began to notice Johnny's strong points, such as language, expression, technology, and science. Maybe his problem was not behavior-oriented at all, maybe he was just bored by not being challenged. I started to sneak in open-ended, creative, whole-language activities into my day, and he would just thrive in these situations. He would dig right into hands-on science activities, creating a closed circuit with a light bulb, wire, and a battery. He became a class leader, a shining star. The only thing that ever held him back was being a late bloomer in reading. But Johnny had overcome that, and now he was showing his full potential—Johnny was a "gifted" child.

At the end of the school year, I was asked to recommend students to move up or down an ability group. I made a bold move and suggested that Johnny get tested for the top class. My magical moment of teaching that year came when I told Johnny he would be tested to move up to the "gifted" class. His reply was simple, yet years later it still sends chills up my spine: "Thank you, Mrs. Boyen, for believing in me. You made me see how smart I really am."

Johnny made it into the top class for fifth grade and proceeded the next year to an honors/college prep middle school. What if I hadn't believed in his potential? Where would he be now? That thought also still sends chills up my spine.

CHAPTER 23

Bob Mauch, 2001

you never know

Lois M. Mauch

Agassiz Middle School
Fargo, North Dakota

was ready to begin the new school year and anxiously awaiting the first meeting with my new students. My goal in teaching physical education is to engage students in physical learning in an innovative way, so they want to remain healthy for a lifetime. However, every teacher manages to get one class that seems to challenge her. That year it was period 6. I had a student by the name of Ellen. She was a bright and energetic redhead and a lead troublemaker in the class. If I said put on blue jerseys, she would not only put on a red one, but she would convince three of her friends to wear red ones too. She refused to do most every activity and dragged other kids with her. It was a very frustrating class to teach. Finally I asked Ellen's parents to come in for a conference. They did, and when I showed them my documentation of Ellen's activity level, they just said, "That is not our Ellen." Frustrated, I just figured there are some students we will help and others we will not. I left it alone. The school year finally ended.

Ellen ran into me that summer. I asked her what she was up to, and her response surprised me. "I'm working out at Courts Plus, a local health club," she said. I remarked, "Good for you, Ellen," and went my way, thinking that maybe I had some effect on her attitude about fitness after all.

September came again, and I was anxious to meet my new students. I knew I would not have Ellen this year; I had put in a request not to have her in my class due to personality conflicts. But during the last period of the day, in walks Ellen. I could not believe my eyes. I got through the first class with Ellen acting quite cordial, then I marched to the office to find out how that "schedule change" took place. The principal pulled out her file and noticed my request. Along with it was a request from her parents to have me as her physical education teacher. I sat there thinking, well, either she is out to get me, or I have made a difference in her life. I decided to risk the latter. We got through that school year just fine together, and I taught Ellen many ways to use technology in physical education to assess her health. It was a wonderful year. After Ellen had gone on to high school, I received a letter from her. Here's what she wrote:

> *I would really like to thank you because you were a great teacher to me. You always made physical education fun, and you taught us new games and strategies. You have affected my life in a positive way by helping me to want to be healthier and more involved in activities. In the beginning, when I was your student, I know I wasn't exactly the greatest kid. But you didn't just give up on me; you knew I could be better, and I was.*
>
> *Having you as a teacher has really been a benefit to my life.*
>
> *Sincerely,*
> Ellen

born to tutor

Hyla Swesnik

Dallas, Texas

I was born to tutor. In seventh grade, there was a blackboard in my bedroom to help me teach math to my friends. By eleventh grade, I was conducting weekly chemistry tutorials, and in college I was math tutor to my entire sorority—eventually branching out and charging for my services.

However, there was one thing I could not tutor: English. I struggled myself with the subject—I could read a story, interpret it, and was great on grammar, but ask me to write an essay and I went into panic mode.

So when I began to teach, it was math, of course. And in addition to teaching, I continued tutoring as well. After several years I was sought out by one of the most insistent mothers I had ever met. She wanted me to tutor her son, Dave, who was about to be a seventh grader at Shelton, a well-known Dallas private school for students with learning disabilities. Not only did she want me to tutor him, but she wanted me to tutor him in vocabulary!

I had many objections. I had never tutored students with learning disabilities; as I repeatedly told her, it is necessary to have a special degree to do so. Plus, I knew nothing about tutoring vocabulary. I had a good vocabulary, but how to teach it? That, I said, is something entirely different. She told me that he needed this tutoring in order to get into a private school when Shelton ended at seventh grade. The tests, which are used as entrance exams, are similar to the SATs but geared for much younger kids. For several years I had been successfully tutoring students for the SATs, but it took courage for me to agree to tutor Dave because I felt inadequate and feared that I might let him down. Never did I dream how life-changing this experience would be for me!

So, here came Dave one summer afternoon. I was supposed to see him three times a week, and after the very first hour, I didn't think I was going to make it. He spoke not one word the entire hour except for a few weak Yeses and Nos. Teaching vocabulary requires at least *some* interaction. For the next three months, he would every once in a while give me a half-grin when I could make the words or tests funny.

I agonized that summer, reading every article I could find about LD teaching. Nothing suggested ways to make the student talk to you. I tried to be funny and get a grin from him—as well as use the repetition necessary for those with learning disabilities.

Dave did not get into private school, but he went to public school and came almost every day for tutoring on a variety of subjects. Although we spent a great deal of time on math, we also went to the library to research term papers and then write them. Finally I learned to do it!

When Dave became a sophomore, it was apparent he was very depressed. During the second semester of Dave's sophomore year, my stepson Josh was diagnosed with ADD without hyperactivity. He and Dave were so alike I immediately called Dave's mother to suggest she have him tested for ADD. After some resistance, she finally agreed and took him to a place that tested via a video game. It was really not a valid test for Dave, but it convinced his mother that he did not have it. By the time he was a junior, he was so depressed that I was worried he would do something to hurt himself. I called his mother once a week to ask that someone else test him. She refused.

I summoned up every ounce of courage I had each time I called Dave's mother, because I thought that I would be fired. After four years, Dave felt like a second son. I didn't want to lose him. One day when I called, his father, a medical doctor, answered the phone, and I was again insistent that he be tested. This time it worked. Dave was tested by a psychologist, was diagnosed with ADD, and was put on Ritalin. It worked so well I rarely saw him again for tutoring. Of course, being part of my family by then, he kept in close contact.

Meanwhile, my SAT tutoring was picking up. I found that I could raise any math score but could not touch the verbal scores unless the student already had a good vocabulary. I began to order vocabulary products that were advertised as highly successful. After spending thousands of dollars, I discovered nothing that worked well. So when Dave was in his senior year, an idea began to form for a product based on our time together.

The idea was to have videos with pictures for every vocabulary word and maybe an animated skit, and workbooks that would explain the words (rather than give dictionary-type definitions), flashcards with pictures repeated, and related synonyms and antonyms. It was a wonderful fantasy, but as I started making lists of synonyms and antonyms, I knew it could never happen because I cannot draw. Then I met an art teacher who became my partner.

It's been five years since Dave went away to college and I began my crusade to get my vocabulary-building products into schools. And, like Dave, I know I will succeed.

CHAPTER 25

Olan Mills

A change of Heart

Anita Gauker

Arbor School
Piscataway, New Jersey

Sometimes, indirect is best. After you've taught for a number of years you are able to sense atypical behavior in a particular student. This was the case with Jimmy, an eleven-year-old boy who was a dependable and conscientious student. At the beginning of March, when outdoor sports were being reactivated, it was obvious that Jimmy was becoming inattentive and withdrawn, and he even missed several days of school. This was not his usual pattern.

One day, his mother picked him up from school at 3:00 dismissal and asked him to wait for her outside the classroom. We discussed Jimmy's recent behavior, and she related the following information: Her husband was a baseball coach who took his work seriously, and their son was on his team. Jimmy was not a good hitter and either struck out or grounded out most of his times at bat. It was so traumatic for him that he began getting sick to his stomach and even throwing up before practice or scheduled games. When she spoke to her son about the situation, he explained that he felt he wasn't living up to his dad's expectations, and he didn't want to ruin the team's chances of winning.

A month later, Jimmy's mom noticed that his pre-game pattern of anxiety had diminished considerably. When she asked him if he was feeling better about playing, he said Yes, because of something he learned about himself during a class discussion. He said that the teacher explained that every person is unique and special, and that each one of us has a gift or talent unlike anyone else's. Jimmy concluded that although he wasn't good at batting, he was a terrific student with excellent math and science skills, and that he needn't excel at everything.

His mother came to thank me for the way I had intervened—without Jimmy even knowing it.

Alison Frost, 2000

And the oscar goes to ...

Alison Frost

Klein High School
Houston, Texas

A s a theater director, I'm always on the lookout for special talents: great voices, interesting looks, and, of course, the ability to act. I'm fortunate enough to teach at a high school filled with kids who excel in these areas—which usually makes for a pretty good musical every January. The year I decided to tackle George Gershwin's *Crazy for You* was a life-changing moment for many of my talented students—many of whom are now embarking upon potentially glamorous careers in the entertainment industry. One cast member, however, probably won't have a glamorous career in his future, but he'll know that for a brief time in his youth he was special.

Born with Williams' syndrome, a rare genetic condition (estimated to occur in 1 in 20,000 births) that causes medical and developmental problems, Brian had attended many of our performances to watch his extremely talented older sister up on the stage. She was cast a lot, so I saw Brian often. Occasionally I make casting decisions in which I know the role will be better for the student than the student is for the role. Theater can change lives. I hoped it would change Brian's. Though he was still a seventh grader, I invited Brian to become a part of *Crazy for You* in the role of a cowboy.

I knew firsthand the power of the theater. During my eighth-grade year, my family left Oklahoma for New Jersey. Mrs. Kelber, my English teacher, privy to my tears about feeling isolated, cast me in a junior high production of *Annie Get Your Gun*. All of a sudden I had an instant family, friends, and a sense of belonging. I even got a laugh. Her casting choice changed my life. Nowadays, when new students enroll in my class I see to it they have someone to sit with at lunch on the very first day. And if they audition, I do my best to find them a role. Over the years I've cast new students, foreign exchange students, and even students with drug and alcohol problems—offering them a more positive extracurricular activity. Now it was Brian's turn.

True to the characteristics of Williams' syndrome, Brian has an incredible sense of rhythm and a great memory. He was able to recite entire passages from plays his sister has been in after only a couple of viewings. So I knew that casting him in *Crazy for You* would be a chance for him to excel and to have fun. He'd have the opportunity to sing and dance and be a part of something unique. Brian would be attending school at Klein a few years down the road, so this was a nice opportunity for him to see the school behind the scenes. Unable even to dress himself, Brian had students assist him with his costumes, choreography, and entrances. The show was a great success, and Brian and the cast received standing ovations from more than 5,000 community members.

Brian has since played a ball boy in *Damn Yankees* (alongside another boy with Down's syndrome) and a party guest in *The Sound of Music*. He continues to take drum lessons and works afternoons at the local grocery store. Having taught Brian in class for the past several years, I feel a true sense of pride in the man that he is becoming.

when there's a wiLL, there's a way

William Sinai

West Valley Occupational Center
Woodland Hills, California

I t was a warm, bright, sunny Monday morning. The young construction worker standing on the twenty-foot-high scaffold was nursing his hangover from the night before. Someone called his name; he turned to respond and stepped forward into thin air. He remembers falling and hitting the concrete below with a thud. He opened his eyes and knew he was in a hospital room. He could not move. His doctor and mother told him that he had severed his spine and was a quadriplegic.

Our Special Services Office asked me if I would accept a student who was a quadriplegic. Scott came into our classroom with the ability to move his head and right hand slightly. He brought with him a special computer program that displayed a keyboard on the screen. He wore a headset that communicated with the computer by infrared radio signals and a mouthpiece that acted as a computer mouse. Scott had a reader to help him with the text and to write the work problems. He was able to use the computer on his own.

Scott also brought with him a sense of humor and a tenacity of purpose. He felt unfulfilled, as he was no longer functioning as a contributing member of society. I taught him accounting theory and helped him develop accounting skills. His family developed a charitable foundation, and he began to work as its accountant. The foundation was set up to help quadriplegics learn to live with their disabilities and to become active members of society.

During the year he was with us, he inspired his classmates and me with his perseverance and determination. I watched as my students became involved in his studies and would find them wandering over to his desk to help him with his work. This was a very fulfilling time for all of us, and I often think back over this time as one of the most rewarding experiences of my thirty-four-year career. As I worked with Scott, I was constantly reminded why I went into teaching—the satisfaction and excitement of touching the future and enabling people to be productive and independent.

CHAPTER 28

Douglas Slater, 2000

Finding your passion

Karen Slater

Arbor School
Piscataway, New Jersey

J esse came to school with very, very low scores and even lower self-esteem. He walked into my Basic Skills class with his head down, hair uncombed, eyes sad. When called upon, he rarely had much to say. It took him a long time to write the answer to even the simplest of questions. When I tried to get him to talk, he would answer in as few words as possible.

His main teacher was a first-year teacher and expressed concerns about him. I told her that even though he was uncommunicative, something told me there was a spark in him yet to be ignited.

He had told me that he liked animals, and one day we happened to be reading about a girl whose mother studied whales. The story told about how they would go to Hawaii together and learn about the humpback whale. Jesse seemed fascinated by it. About a week later he brought me some books that he had taken out of the library about whales. He began to tell me all about the different types of whales and how they differed. He was able to go back in the books and share passages that he had read. This was remarkable for a child who hadn't shared much of anything before.

I asked if he was willing to share this with the other children. To my amazement, he said Yes. And suddenly Jesse was in front of the other children, confidently talking about the beluga whale and the killer whale and giving details about their size, lifestyles, and how they differed.

It was as if he had been transformed; he was so excited to share this information! Within the next few weeks, he began to write with greater ease and read and speak with more confidence.

When the children subsequently wrote stories about what they wanted to be when they grew up, he said, "I want to be a marine biologist." At the end of the year, he scored well enough to get out of the Basic Skills class. He has many more years of school to go, but he still wants to be a marine biologist. I tell him that I want to be the first to congratulate him when he gets his degree.

tears of truth

Kimberly Stewart

Dodgen Middle School
Marietta, Georgia

It was my fifth year of teaching, and I felt settled and secure in my role as a middle school teacher. Then I encountered Chin. A small Korean boy with an angelic face and porcelain skin, Chin looked much younger than his eleven years. After only a few weeks of school, we received the news that Chin's mother had died of a heart attack. Saddened and concerned, my teammate and I attended the funeral. At the funeral, I discovered that an elderly grandmother who kept foster children had adopted Chin several years before; she was the only mother he had ever known. My heart was ripped apart as I watched Chin sobbing while he threw his arms over her casket.

Eventually, Chin returned to school. I made every attempt to make him feel safe, secure, and loved in my classroom. I was extremely sensitive to his plight, and he could probably read the concern in my eyes as he entered my class each day. I tried to bring him as much happiness as was possible under the circumstances.

Slowly, Chin changed from the sweet, shy little boy I loved into someone quite different. He began to act out in class and was often disruptive. In retrospect, I may have been too patient with his misbehavior at first, but I knew he needed to be treated tenderly. When I finally corrected Chin, he responded with disrespect. He often rolled his eyes or ignored me. I tried my entire repertoire of behavior management techniques, only to find that Chin's behavior became even worse.

Baffled, I consulted with Chin's other teachers to see what they were doing with him now that he had changed so drastically. I was dismayed to learn that in every other class, Chin was still the sweet and shy child I had once known. Embarrassed, I began to question everything about my competence as a teacher. I had always felt a sense of pride at my ability to connect with even the most difficult students; I was known as the teacher who was able to reach the kids no one else could.

I felt even more bewildered when I watched Chin look at me. His eyes glared with hatred. No one had ever looked at me that way before. I know that we teachers cannot expect to be adored by every one of our students. Indifference I could have handled, but hatred? When I tried talking to him alone, he refused to discuss the situation. When I asked him why he was behaving this way, he had no response. He refused to go to the counselor.

I found myself dreading his class each day. What would Chin do to destroy my lesson? I lay awake at night wondering what I did to cause this child to act this way toward me, and I felt torn by my feelings of frustration, concern, and anger. Chin, however, knew nothing of my internal struggle. I continued to treat him with patience and kindness, although I became much firmer when disciplining him.

One day I was in the middle of one of those lessons when everything was going beautifully, when you can see the spark in every student's eyes. Things couldn't have been more perfect, and Chin realized it. He decided to lean his chair back and stick his feet inside the desk, only to have them get stuck. He fell over in his chair, tipping over the desk and spilling its contents all over the floor. I couldn't blame the students for laughing, but I was infuriated that Chin had destroyed yet another lesson. I asked a teacher to watch my class, and I escorted Chin to the counselor.

That afternoon, I received the answer to my weeks of endless questions. The counselor came to talk to me after she spent the afternoon with Chin. "He hates me," I remarked disdainfully.

She replied, "Yes, he does hate you," she replied, "but not for the reasons you might think. You see, you remind him of his mother. I know you're much younger than she was, but it's the way you try to take care of him. He even said it's the way you smell. He has been trying to make you be mean to him. He can't stand being around you because it just hurts too much. He's been crying all afternoon."

That day, I learned my single greatest lesson as a teacher. I learned to never give up on any child, no matter how frustrating the situation. And, I learned that those children who are the most difficult to love are the ones who need love the most.

Incidentally, Chin began to see the counselor regularly after that "breakthrough day." We slowly rebuilt our relationship, and once again, he became a joy to have in class.

Jesse A. Bravo

memories

Larry Bordeaux

Foothill High School
Sacramento, California

E ach year my seniors study *Macbeth*. One of the assignments is always a recitation by each of the students of an important speech from the play. Every year we set a goal of completing the recitation assignment without errors, but that goal has never quite been achieved. Half in jest, I plead with my students to give me the opportunity to hear an entire class recite the speech without a single mistake before I retire.

This year, to my (and the students') delight and astonishment, each person eloquently recited the speech without one error! Afterward, they told they had secretly made a class project out of my request for perfect recitations and had practiced innumerable times to ensure that it happened.

CHAPTER 31

Arden Photographers, 2000

survivor

Mary McGrann

New York City Board of Education
Staten Island, New York

was just out of college and looking for my first real teaching job. I had been hired as a substitute teacher, but I hoped that real teaching was about more than that. I was ready for the good stuff, the stuff that lives and dreams are made of.

The principal, who had been kind enough to hire me as a regular substitute, called me into her office for a meeting. I had no idea what this was about. I walked inside and found a few other young women who also were searching for their first real job. A diminutive older gentleman was sitting in the principal's office. It became clear that he would conduct this meeting. I don't know if I ever knew his name. I realize now that he was a special messenger in my life and that he guided me to who I have become since.

"Ladies," he began. "There are not too many teaching jobs available these days." I began to feel defeated and started to wonder what else I could possibly do with my life. "However," he continued, "if each one of you goes back to school and pursues a master's degree in special education, I can guarantee that every one of you will immediately be placed in a permanent job."

Special education? What did they do in those rooms? How did they reach the unreachable and teach the unteachable? Panic swept over me. Even more shocking was that I found myself raising my hand to volunteer to follow this unknown path! A force greater than myself was leading me to my destiny.

I can still recall the first special education class I subbed in. I was so terrified! I am sure they raked me over the coals, but I didn't even realize it. I had survived and with each passing moment I learned what my newly found population had always known—that life exists after humiliation. I learned that a tomorrow always follows today. I learned how to get myself back up on my feet after being knocked down. I learned that the bravest people in the world have known incredible fear and have lived through it. I learned that crying is okay and that laughing is even better. And I have learned how to love and respect in a deeper way than I ever dreamed possible.

So many students have left their footprints on my heart and soul. So many have opened my eyes when I didn't realize they were shut. I have welcomed new arrivals, and sobbed when saying good-bye each June. I have learned how to love and how to let go. I have learned that teaching parallels the life cycle unlike any other job.

There are many moments of uncertainty in teaching. Often I wondered if I was on the right track. I hoped I was making a connection. I hoped and prayed that I could touch lives as the children touched mine. The results of our work as teachers often take a long time to become apparent. I was in one of those crises of uncertainty when a letter arrived in my mailbox from a former student.

The letter was from a young girl that I had taught when she was hospitalized after attempting suicide. She had been alone in the world after being abandoned by her parents. She didn't know what grade she was in. She was quite delayed academically, but amazingly, she was always smiling. She had suffered many kinds of abuses by grown-ups who were supposed to be there to help her. Yet, she was still willing to trust again. She had started several fires in group homes and foster homes as a cry for help. She endured numerous operations for a medical condition. Yet, she was a survivor.

Her letter, which arrived on my birthday, began by saying that she was now a nurse, a mother to three beautiful daughters, a homeowner, and a loving wife. She wrote to say "Thank you" to me for making her feel special and smart and for always believing in her. Tears poured out of my eyes as goose bumps broke out all over my body. She had made it! And she took the time to let me know that I had helped make that possible.

Erik and Rich Johnson

Mrs. J's Little Book of Instructions for Life

Susan Johnson

Herricks High School
New Hyde Park, New York

I t was a morning class of ninth graders, five years ago. The course was called "Introduction to Occupations," but it was really an introduction to business topics. I was just about to hand out a quiz when I noticed Geeti silently crying in the back of the room. Her friend Raji ran up to tell me that Geeti's dog had died the day before. I insisted that Geeti forget about the quiz. What was so important about a quiz that it couldn't be taken another time? She had something more important to do—grieve for her Buster. I let her go to the girls' room while the rest of the class scribbled out their answers.

The night before that class, I had been cruising around on the Internet, trying to find information on a certain soap opera star who designed clothing. In my search, I came across a site about saying good-bye to a pet who has passed on. I remembered thinking, "Why the heck is this site showing up in my search?" Now, of course, we know why.

After the class, I had a prep period scheduled. Instead of grading those quizzes, I took Geeti to a computer in the library. I again searched for that soap opera star, and again I got the pet-grieving site. Geeti sat down and wrote a letter to her special friend and said good-bye. I waited outside until she was finished, and then gave her a pass to her next class.

When she graduated last year, Geeti gave me a pair of silver salt-and-pepper shakers. The note attached read:

> *Some people come into our lives and quickly leave, while some stay*
> *awhile leaving footprints in our souls, making memories that the*

heart preserves. Mrs. Johnson, your footprints have left their mark in my life and will remain there forever and always. You are my number one example of strength, compassion, and dedication. I love your warmth, your charm, and your glow. I know I could've given you something conventional, but convention suits neither one of us and so I've decided to give you a very special gift. I'm giving you "teacher shoes" as a symbol of all that you have done for me, all that you've taught me, and all that you've imprinted on me.

Love,

Geeti

The class of 2000, Geeti's class, asked me to be their speaker at graduation. I had put together their prom, attended plays, recitals, and games during the previous four years. I even squeezed in a bilateral mastectomy and chemotherapy. I have found that the more I give, the better I feel. And I always have my sixty-five students and ex-students on my buddy list to encourage or make laugh.

This is the graduation speech I gave at Herricks High School in June 2000:

> I would like to say "Thank you" to the class of 2000 for asking me to speak today. I feel very honored that you chose me to speak. I have been a teacher at Herricks for twenty-five years. I thought I would prepare a little booklet of lessons called "Mrs. J's Little Book of Instructions for Life." So let's get started before the bell rings for dismissal.
>
> Lesson One: Don't be a potato—a couch potato. Don't let life pass by

in front of you. Try new things. My family moved right before it was time for me to start high school. Since I didn't know too many people when I was in high school, I was very shy. If a boy talked to me, I would melt on the floor. I made the decision that when I went to Albany State University, I would be a different person. I would go to all the plays, protest marches, special lectures, mixers, all-night movie fests that I could, and I dragged my four roommates with me. It was hard at first, but the more I became involved, the shyness wore away, and I made a lot of friends and learned so much about life. I even talked to boys! As you walk out of here today, vow to experience some of the wonderful things in life. You should always be a student.

Lesson Two: Tickle Me Elmo. (I put a large Elmo doll on the lectern.) This lesson is easy to understand. Laugh as much as you can—always. My dad recently passed on. Everyone loved my dad. He was always joking around and teasing and laughing. When he died, I decided that his gift of laughter was given to me. I now like to joke around and tease. He was right; laughter makes everything easier to handle. I still walk into the oncologist's office wearing all my "queen" jewelry. The staff treats me like royalty, and we laugh and laugh.

Lesson Three: Ewok! (I placed a large Ewok on the lectern.) Ewoks are little creatures from the *Star Wars* movies. In my classes we turned a nasty four-letter word that sometimes would appear written on a book or a desk into the word *Ewok*.

Let me put it another way: When life sends you lemons, make lemonade. I have had quite a few lemons in my life recently. My husband had to leave teaching here at Herricks and go on disability. My dad passed on suddenly. Last year I developed breast cancer. Yet this year I had the greatest teaching year I have ever had. In part it was because this graduating class is so generous with their love. I took my illness and made lemonade. I pray that each of you will have the recipe for lemonade in your lives.

Lesson Four: A boa! (I wrap a large purple feather boa around myself.) Yes, I have a feather boa. I recently read a quote from an author named Anne Stuart. It goes like this: "But I can tell you the secret of living a great life. And that is a feather boa—it's all you need. Why, you ask? It's because no one can ever be pompous, tragic, and desperate or take him or herself seriously if they're wearing a pink feather boa. You have to loosen up and laugh at yourself and the total absurdity of life. And then there's no way it can destroy you."

When I finished chemo last summer, I lost my hair. I didn't wear a wig but some funny hats unless it was too warm. There is a picture in your yearbook of me with very little hair. Some of you think that was very brave. But in the whole picture of life, does my hair make me the person I am? Perhaps if more people didn't wear wigs, we would realize how many people have cancer and work harder to find the causes and a cure. So if you fall on your face in the mud, laugh.

When I was first teaching, it was at the junior high that is now the community center. I had my class on the second floor. There are very long windows in that building and they are very low. I had club meetings in that room. I would constantly tell the kids to stay away from the window because I was afraid that they would fall out. One day I was distracted by someone at the door when I heard everyone screaming. I ran over to the window. Everyone shouted out, "Charlie fell out! Charlie fell out!" Sure enough, I looked out the window and there was Charlie lying on the ground looking like this. . . . He sure didn't look like he was breathing. So I started screaming, "I told you not to go near the windows!" Of course, it was a prank. They had set the whole thing up. Charlie had run down the stairs and planted himself outside the window. What do you think my reaction was? I laughed.

Lesson Five: Get a life! Don't make yourself a slave to a bigger house, a bigger bonus, or a bigger paycheck. Send e-mails to friends or call Grandma and Grandpa. Don't go to clubs every weekend. Try building a house for Habitat for Humanity. You'd be surprised how many people you would meet doing that. Or how about coaching a soccer team for a few months in the fall? I truly believe that those who give generously to others receive back a thousand times more.

This class is well on the way to great things. Not because you have the skills and knowledge to succeed, which you do, but because you are generous with your love and time and gifts. Stay that way. Make your life uniquely yours.

Stand out. You don't have to dress like everyone else. On the other hand, you don't have to dress like me either! One of you recently gave me this quote: "Some people come into our lives and quickly leave, while some stay awhile leaving footprints in our souls, making memories that the heart preserves." That's how I feel about this graduating class. Now go out there and live, laugh, and learn. You have left your footprints on my heart forever. There will be a quiz on this material next Monday, which is business test day. Thank you.

CHAPTER 33

Dan Painter Photography, 1999

That Ah-Ha Moment

Mimi Roth

Northwood Hills Elementary
Dallas, Texas

I teach first grade in a suburban public school. Throughout my career, I have taught in inner-city, private, and ethnically diverse schools. One thing I have come to realize is that all six-year-olds have much in common. They come to school in August knowing letter sounds and maybe, if we're lucky, a few written words, and leave in May reading books and writing stories and feeling like they have the world in the palm of their hands. And of course, they do!

I love teaching children how to read and write. Each August I look out at my class of twenty-two students and see lost little faces looking back at me. As we go over and over the sounds of the letters and gradually put them with vowels to form words, I see the delight in their faces. There is nothing so exciting as the look on the face of a children as he begins reading his first book. Try as hard as they can, they are unable to wipe the grins off their faces as they read their first words.

I remember talking to one student years after he was in my class. Evan was in high school at the time, and we were sitting around his kitchen table. It was always so rewarding to keep up with students long after they had left my class and ventured out into the great big world. That day, as we spoke with others his age, Evan proudly looked over at me, exclaiming, "You were the one who taught me to read—she was my first grade teacher." I don't know who was the proudest one at that table—Evan for being able to introduce his "old" teacher or me for looking at a previous student now grown and matured. I know that I had an impact on him, for that very same day he went into his bedroom closet and came out with the remnants of a bulletin board from my first grade class. Crumpled, faded, and a little torn, this first grade memory had stood the test of time. It was a reminder of a time filled with learning, wonderment, and awe, when this young man felt good about himself and the world around him.

Yes, they come into my world as nonreaders and leave with the whole world at their feet, because I have helped them learn to read. By doing my part, I hope I have been the first of many teachers to open up their world of opportunity.

CHAPTER 34

Danielle Crane, 2000

snoopy, Linus, Lucy, and Nancy

Debi Crane

Pine Creek High School
Colorado Springs, Colorado

received my bachelor's degree in special education, in the area of working with emotionally disturbed students. I was hired, along with a full-time teacher's aide, to work with only one student in a self-contained setting. We were in a building with about thirty-five to forty mentally retarded students, because there wasn't any place for us in the regular school.

I figured the student I was assigned to must be incredibly disturbed to need two people to work full-time with her. As it was, they had hired the two of us in hope of building the program. My student's name was Nancy. Nancy was a tiny, thin fourth-grade girl who had a short shaggy haircut that always hung in her face. She was always angry; she held her little body rigid, her hands at her sides in fists, and would make angry faces, saying things like, "I'm gonna knock your block off; I just wanna kick you across the room." She would say this in voices that imitated characters from the Charlie Brown comic strip *Peanuts*. An extremely good artist, she would also draw *Peanuts* comic strips, with her brother and herself as characters.

Her anger was mainly vented toward her brother, of whom she was very jealous. In her eyes, he was a pest. She became Lucy in her scripts, and Lucy's little brother Linus—the one with the blanket—became her brother. In one strip, the first panel showed her in her bedroom looking angry. In the second, she would make a statement to the effect of, "When I see my little brother, I am going to clobber him." The third would be the confrontation with the little brother. By the fourth, she would have kicked him like a football, sending him flying out of the picture. The last would show a very satisfied smile on the face of Lucy.

Back in those days I made home visits and realized she had a very loving family. Nancy just didn't realize how much attention a newborn or younger sibling might need from his parents. Time went on, and as Nancy got better we talked a lot about younger siblings. I began to work with her through cartoons. I would sit down with her to work on the comic strips; I would draw my own but put in positive situations (my drawings were stick figures). I would bring in the *Peanuts* comic strips that showed funny positive moments, and I brought in information on Charles Schulz. Her cartoons changed to more positive stories: playing with her brother, going for family drives, reading to her brother.

The pivotal moment came after I sent to Charles Schulz a copy of his published biography along with a note about Nancy, enclosing a positive comic she had done about him. I asked if he would sign the book and mail it to her. A month later I received a phone call from Nancy's mom. She told me that Nancy had received an autographed book from Mr. Schulz with a short message to Nancy encouraging her art talent. It was magic, and Nancy had totally turned around by the end of the school year.

CHAPTER 35

Life Touch Studios, 1999

who's Helping whom?

Lana Croft

Gladneo Parker Elementary
Galveston, Texas

had returned to the teaching profession after being in the banking world for fifteen years. I knew that with my experience and maturity I had a lot to offer. I had genuine love and respect for my students, and I felt fortunate to receive their love on a daily basis. However, I didn't develop the compassion I've seen other teachers demonstrate until three angels in my class taught me the lesson I needed to learn.

My first special student, David, explained to his fellow fifth graders and their teacher what it is like to have epilepsy. He explained how it felt to wear a helmet all day at school, to have seizures several times a day, and to come to school with a Labrador service dog who helped him during his day. I had never seen a seizure and did not possess the tiniest shred of confidence that I would do the right thing. Of course, the students were upset the first time they saw our friend have a seizure. After that they were so helpful and so kind that they showed me how to handle a situation where only love and compassion are needed. David and our school nurse had taught me what I needed to do physically to help him; the students had shown me how to respond emotionally.

My next lesson in compassion came the following year. Justin was already loved by others, but I was worried that because he had Down's syndrome, he would not make good progress in my classroom. What if I didn't know enough to help him learn? His parents reassured me that Justin demonstrated his love of others and his love for learning every day. My heart will never be the same since sharing the world through Justin's eyes.

My third lesson in compassion came the next year. Meredith was in a wheelchair and was often absent. I was again concerned that she might not progress or that I might not know how to help her when she needed it. Once again her loving parents and my loving students showed me what was important. The fifth graders argued over who would sit next to Meredith and who would eat lunch next to her. "Mrs. Croft, it's my turn to push Meredith out to the playground!"

I came to fifth grade with a passion for teaching children. Now, because of these children, I'm learning to grow a heart filled with compassion.

CHAPTER 36

Myrna Eddison, 2000

KiDS ARe PeopLe TOO

Jim Eddison

Toronto, Ontario

T hroughout my teaching career people would often say to me, "I don't envy you. I couldn't go into a classroom every day and face those thirty little monsters. You're a very brave man!" I would always shake my head and smile. I wasn't brave, and I wasn't dealing with monsters. For me teaching was never an ordeal, never an onerous task. For me, every day in the classroom was a joy. I had fun, the children had fun, and together we enjoyed success. I have always enjoyed teaching, and I believe the majority of my students have enjoyed learning.

My teaching/learning journey began in an elementary school in the dock area of Liverpool, England. My first class was made up of forty-two boys, and I was not at all confident that I would be able to manage a class of very tough students. The headmaster provided me with a bamboo cane, with instructions on how and when to use it. After a few days of testing the waters, I made a significant discovery. These tough kids did not need the cane—they responded positively to humor. I was able to establish a rapport with these boys because they appreciated my sense of humor. This was a discovery that was to stand me in good stead for the rest of my career. I could do my job and have fun at the same time.

After a three-year apprenticeship in this school, I was ready for a new challenge so I immigrated to Canada. For the next twenty-nine years I taught in a variety of inner-city schools in Toronto. Throughout those years I was continually learning. I learned from principals, from teachers, and from support personnel, but my most important lessons were learned from children. One day I inadvertently used the world *adults* when I meant "people." A very polite eight-year-old raised her hand and said, "Kids are people too!" This gentle reminder made me more aware of how to treat my students. I had always shown respect toward my students, but from that time on I was ever vigilant. We must all remember that kids are people. They have valid feelings, they have dignity, and they deserve respect. We tend to be very aware of physical abuse, but we sometimes disregard the damage wrought by verbal and emotional abuse.

Another lesson I learned from the children was to sometimes allow the kid inside me to come out and have fun. Teachers need to connect with kids if they are to be successful. When a teacher lets his "kid" out, the children recognize a kindred spirit and the basis for mutual respect is established.

For many years I taught students with special needs, and during this time, I learned more about the importance of self-esteem. Most of my students had experienced failure throughout their school lives, and I realized that I could not teach them until they believed that they could succeed. My main focus at the beginning of each year was to boost self-esteem. I gave each student a nickname, which always included his or her proper name. These nicknames were usually either rhyming or alliterative. One year I taught a class that included Slick Nick (Nicholas); Mayday, Mayday, Mayday (May); Ready Robert (Robert); and Justin Time (Justin). I always sought their permission to use these names, and I was never refused. They felt important because this name was unique to them. There might have been another Nicholas in the school but there was only one Slick Nick. Every child was important to me, and I let him or her know it at every possible opportunity.

After thirty-two years, I retired from full-time teaching. Within six months I was back in the classroom—as a volunteer! I was asked by a friend to help out with a Play Day at the school across the road from my house. I eagerly agreed to be involved, and off I went. I spent one day with the kids and I was hooked again! I realized that I still had a lot to offer and that this school had a lot to offer me. I spend part of every day in a wonderful Grade 1 classroom with forty students and two excellent young teachers, and I am still learning more about teaching and about young children. One day a charming little girl asked me, "Mr. Eddison, why are you always smiling?" I answered, "Because I am having so much fun!"

Return to the Basics

Bob Coleman

Oakville, Connecticut
National Teachers Hall of Fame, 1994

I have been asked to write you a letter welcoming you into a career that I enjoyed for thirty-seven years. I wondered how anyone could possibly explain the joys and frustrations of teaching to someone just embarking on such a complicated journey. Let me be honest about this before you read any further: If you want real answers, don't look to me. My answers are mine, not yours. You will find your own answers in your own experiences. Those answers will change with each new class you meet. Each of us must discover the true meaning of teaching in our own understanding of ourselves and of our relationships with the students we meet.

My students feel I taught them more than they ever taught me. Nothing could be further from the truth.

Let me tell you about Tracy. She was my very first student. I was in college, reluctantly meeting a requirement for community service. Tracy was severely retarded. She was also classified as incorrigible. She was forty-seven years old when I first met her. She had been confined in a prison cottage in a southern state training school for thirty-four years. Tracy had a terrible temper. At thirteen years old, she had pushed her mother out of a window. When her mother died as a result of the fall, the courts placed her in a huge school for the retarded, and the school in turn placed Tracy in the jail cottage, where she had remained all those years.

There were three solid steel doors that had to be unlocked before I could reach Tracy's fetid cell. Each door required two keys. Finally I was locked inside Tracy's cell for the 45-minute class. A matron stood guard outside the cell door. Tracy sat on the corner of a urine-soaked cot with her head down and shoulders stooped. Her matted hair hung over her eyes. Her face was blotched and bloated. Her arms drooped at her sides, Neanderthal-like. The toilet located in the corner of the cell had overflowed so often that a green scum covered the floor. That was my first classroom.

As a volunteer teacher, my task was to prepare Tracy for her First Communion. I was to teach her that God made her and loved her. Our weekly classes went on for two years. We both began to look forward to them. I was the only visitor that Tracy ever had. After six months, the matron disappeared. After a year, the cell door was left unlocked. Eventually, we held class in a visitors' room near the main entrance.

Tracy loved to play a game we made up. I would ask, "Who made the grass?" Tracy would reply, "God made the grass." Then I would ask, "Why did God make the grass?"

Tracy would respond, "Because He loves me." I would ask, "Who made the trees and the rivers and the sun?" until I ran out of things. Each time Tracy would answer that God made them. Tracy would wait for me to ask, "Why did He make them?" and she would reply, "Because God loves Tracy."

The final question was always, "Tracy, who made you?" And Tracy would giggle and answer, "God made Tracy." She would never wait for me to ask why. She couldn't hold it in. "Because He loves Tracy," she would rush to say.

I received permission to have our final class outside. It was the first time Tracy had been out of her "cottage" in her thirty-four years at the school. Tracy came alive. She reached down and rubbed her hands through the lush grass and asked me, "What is this?" When I told her, "Grass," she began to twirl and roll and cry in happiness. Her eyes sparkled in a way I had never seen before. She took my hands and we danced together. She began to ask me our question game. I took her lines and she took my lines. It was so natural. She became the teacher. Her final question was, "Who made Bob?" I answered, "God made Bob." She interrupted to say, "Because Tracy loves Bob."

I learned more from Tracy than Tracy ever learned from me. I learned that not everyone knows what grass is, and a good teacher shouldn't assume that everyone does. I learned that there must be a joy in the relationship between teacher and student before real learning can take place in either. I learned that which one was the teacher really wasn't that important as long as both learned. I learned the joy of teaching is allowing oneself to be taught.

Most important, I learned the joy of discovering in my classes the people who will help to shape the present and give hope to the future.

Whenever I think of Tracy and the others, my mind wanders to that old story about the frog. I'm sure you remember it. The frog was once a handsome prince whom a wicked witch had turned into an ugly wart-covered creature. Only the kiss of a beautiful maiden could change him back. So there he sat, an unkissed prince trapped inside a frog. But in children's stories and in teaching miracles do happen. One day a beautiful maiden grabbed up the frog and planted a huge smack right on his lips. Suddenly he was a handsome prince again. And you know the rest—they lived happily ever after.

That is what teaching is all about. We are part of that miracle. We are part of that process that makes princes out of frogs. The question to ask yourself is, "Which would you rather be—a prince or a frog?"

Sheila Moure-Brooker, 2001

A Life That Matters

Gerard Brooker, Ed.D.

Bethel, Connecticut

National Teachers Hall of Fame, 1998

It was in the aftermath of the death of one of my students that I came to know more fully how effective I could be in my students' lives. I had known Jim for five years before he died. A talented writer and wonderful person, he helped write radio commercials for a campaign I had started to help abandoned children. The campaign was successful, and Jim later went off to the University of Missouri to study journalism.

Sadly, he developed lung cancer and died during his sophomore year. It was with a very heavy heart that I went to his funeral. As I was offering my condolences to his family, Jim's dad asked me to step aside for a private talk. He told me that two weeks before he died, Jim went through his memorabilia to select a few items for burial with him. His dad told me that he chose five things, including an essay he had written in my class years before. I had written a note on it, which I had hoped would be empowering to Jim. In it, I encouraged him, as I had before and have since to many others, to believe in himself and in his talents and to develop them to the fullest. He chose to take this note with him across the Great Divide. I was deeply moved. And I was grateful for the extraordinary gift that Jim gave to me that day. His wonderful gesture gave the teacher in me a most powerful insight, one that would change my life: what a tremendous opportunity for impacting students' lives the profession of teaching offered to me—to you.

In the Book of Hasidim it says that in the end we will not be asked, "Why were you not Moses, the Savior?" Rather, we each will be asked why we were not ourselves. In my case, I shall be asked, "Why were you not Gerard Brooker, the teacher?" I have tried to lead my life so that I can answer, "I was."

ALL YOU EVEr NEED TO KNOW

Antonio A. Fierro

El Paso, Texas
Texas State Teacher of the Year, 1997

A ugust was the start of our school year, and this one promised to be just as exciting as all the rest. The week before, I had been anxiously getting ready. The bulletin boards were almost done, and the kindergarten room was starting to come alive. My class roster had just been delivered to me, so I had plenty of time to begin writing down my students' names on color-coded sentence strips. Bart, Holly, Sally, Wendy, Melissa, Todd, Michael were names that I read off the list. As I began writing the names, I wondered what kind of year we would all have and what kind of experiences we would all share. I never anticipated that this particular group of students would touch my heart forever.

The first day of school I always had my criers. I should have known something was going to be special about this year, because this time the criers were the parents dropping off their five-year-olds for the first day of school. After the children reassured their parents that everything would be all right, they sent them off to work, and the school year began. And what a year it was!

About one month into school I accidentally hit my knee on one of our classroom tables. Following a period of hopping around holding on to my knee and complaining about the excruciating pain, Todd said to me, "Mr. Fierro, you're just a baby." There was so much conviction in his voice that I didn't know whether to laugh or be embarrassed. That year, as a classroom and an extended family of sorts, we experienced the death of a classmate together, arrivals of new siblings together, but most of all, we celebrated life and learning together.

Learning took place at all levels of my students' cognitive and social domains. We all know that as teachers we have to tie in all learning to our students' lives, thus making all learning relevant and real. With this class, our lessons always went beyond learning. They found their ways into personal growth and social awareness that still exist in all of us today, years later.

Recently, I ran into Todd's parents. They told me that Todd is coming along very well and is on his way to middle school. However, one thing stands out about him and the rest of that "special" class: their dedication to each other, and the friendship and respect they have for one another even today.

And, what about that "baby" comment Todd made way back when? Well, a couple of months ago I happened to see the old group at the school library. After visiting with them for a while, Melissa, who used to dance a mean Humpty-Dumpty, suggested a group picture. Michael, who has been and probably always will be prepared for anything, had a camera. Everyone gathered around me, and I suggested that I sit on a chair, as many of the students are either my height or taller now. Todd asked if someone was going to sit on my lap. All the kids looked at each other, confused. When no one answered, Todd quickly sat himself down on one of my legs, and Melissa followed suit on the other. So Todd, you were calling me a baby? No matter how old or how tall my former students are, they will always be my kindergarten kids.

CHAPTER 40

Diane Jarvis Jones, 2000

what goes around comes around

Shelley Hrdlitschka

North Vancouver, British Columbia

Ben would stand quietly in the doorway of my classroom after I'd dismissed the students. I'll never forget him—wide-eyed, tiny, intense, and exceptionally introspective for his ten years. I'd invite him in and put him to work hanging artwork or stacking chairs. I hadn't ever been his teacher, but had met him while coaching the high school track and field team. We'd become friends, and he would come to my classroom to talk. I always wished I'd had some counseling skills to fall back on, but all I could do was listen.

He would tell me, way back then, about the disruptive kid he'd been during the primary grades. I was surprised to hear it, but then he explained how his Grade 5 teacher was helping him to turn his life around. Ben spent a lot of time talking about this gifted teacher and how skillfully he'd taught Ben to control his temper. In fact, Ben was so grateful to this man that he declared he would grow up and become a teacher so that he, too, could help troubled kids.

I've since left teaching to pursue a dream of writing children's books. Now, after publishing four of them, I'm often back in the classroom sharing my writing experiences. Not long ago I was invited to speak at the school where I once was a teacher. Before my presentation, a young man approached me and introduced himself. It was Ben, who had followed his dream and was now teaching at the school.

After my author presentation, Ben approached me again, but he was clearly uncomfortable this time. In that moment I could see the little boy again, squirming, wanting to share something. Then he let it spill. He told me that he's always wanted to thank me for taking the time to listen to him all those years ago. Such a small thing, I thought, but then he explained how he remembers our afternoon sessions when one of his own students needs to talk. When he feels impatient he recalls how he, too, once needed an unbiased adult to talk with, and it helps him to be a better listener.

What goes around, comes around.

CHAPTER 41

Robbie Batts

A Lesson in Humanity

Cheri Thanos

Dallas, Texas

During my twenty-two years as an educator, I have had countless wonderful, fulfilling, humorous, and gratifying experiences. However, I would like to share my most memorable experience: when I, the teacher, along with my eighth graders, became a student of Mr. George Brent, a Holocaust survivor. This profound life lesson will stay with me forever.

Each year, my Language Arts 8 students studied the Holocaust extensively, through the reading of *The Diary of Anne Frank, Daniel's Story* by Carol Matas, and *Night* by Elie Weisel. Although *Night* is a very graphic and disturbing account of the author's experiences in a concentration camp during the Holocaust, I felt that middle school students were at an age when they could learn about the devastating effects of hate. Middle school students are very concerned with justice and fairness. Through their study, I wanted the students to understand the meaning of compassion for others and to respect each other's differences.

As a culminating event, I scheduled a field trip to the Dallas Center for Holocaust Studies. This is when my students and I first met Mr. Brent. Although his talk was very powerful and the audience was riveted on his every word, it wasn't until he spoke of his love for playing his violin as a young teen that they bonded.

When there was evidence of war in Hungary, his violin was given to a non-Jewish friend for safekeeping. Then, when the Nazis invaded Budapest, young George was no longer allowed to attend the public school or continue his lessons. Because many of my Montessori students played in the orchestra and aspired to go on to the Arts Magnet High School, they understood his loss. During the question-and-answer segment of the program, the students gathered around to ask him many questions. He was patient and loving toward each and every one. Many hugged him as we left, and I knew there was a special bond that would never be broken.

When the students and I returned to school, the first thing they asked me was if the orchestra students could have a special concert to honor Mr. Brent. Of course, all of the students wanted to participate. I told them that I would first speak to the orchestra director and then would call the museum to find out if they could contact Mr. Brent and ask him to phone me. Of course, when I spoke to him, he said that he would be delighted to come to our school! The most difficult question I needed to ask him was the request made by my students: Would he bring his violin and play for us?

Then the planning began.... I have never witnessed so much cama-raderie among my students. Their enthusiasm was contagious.

When the day finally arrived, the concert was unique in that there were more orchestra members on stage than people in the audience. The audience was Mr. Brent; his wife of fifty years, Anita; Frieda Soble, who at the time was Executive Director of the Dallas Holocaust Museum; my eighth grade students not in the orchestra; a few parents and teachers, and me. The students played beautifully. Two played solos. Then George Brent climbed on stage and played "Ave Maria" and "Kol Nidre"—his violin had been returned to him in the late 1950s in the United States. There wasn't a dry eye in the house.

I have never felt so moved and proud to be an educator. My so-called lesson went far beyond anything I could have imagined. I, too, was awak-ened to the value of human love and compassion. Although George Brent had suffered the devastating effects of hate, he clearly spoke a message of love and tolerance. He changed all of our lives in a profound way forever.

George became our adopted grandfather and continued to visit our school and speak to subsequent eighth grade classes until his death. I feel blessed to have had the opportunity to honor him, as he was truly a gifted teacher.

CHAPTER 42

Jeanne Burkhardt, 2000

it's a matter of attitude

Ross M. Burkhardt

Las Cruces, New Mexico
National Teachers Hall of Fame, 1998

W hen I recall some of the best moments I've had as a teacher, invariably Max comes to mind. At that time, my official responsibility was teaching English and social studies to a team of forty-five eighth graders on Long Island, New York.

Max was school phobic. He had missed much of his seventh grade year with upset stomachs and other vague maladies. He was not one of the world's best students—far from it. When he arrived in my eighth grade classroom, his writing skills were, to put it kindly, abominable. My students were expected to write every day in both English and social studies, and Max was no exception. During the year he composed a plethora of pieces: journal entries, letters, reports, reactions, narratives, poems, interior monologues, personal essays, newspaper articles, and editorials. This variety and volume of writing tasks gave Max numerous opportunities to express himself by selecting topics of interest to him; he also had to prepare pieces for publication on a regular basis. Slowly but incrementally, in a supportive environment, Max found his voice as a writer.

The year's writing activities culminated in late spring, with a four-week unit during which each student produced an individual magazine on a self-selected topic. Max's was titled—no surprise to those who knew him—*Boogie Skate!* Max was a "thrasher" and had already written reams about the thrills and chills of skateboarding. He loved the individual magazine project because he could celebrate himself as he explored his passion.

During a team meeting at the end of the year, I asked Max and his classmates to identify three significant learning experiences they had had that year. Max's opening statement to the assembled team was a stunner: "I learned that I am a writer," he asserted. While no one would ever confuse him with Hemingway, Max in fact had become a writer, and he had published evidence to support his claim. How far he had come in a year!

What interested me, though, was why? Why did Max feel he could make that claim? What had I done that enabled Max to declare himself a successful learner—a writer—after his disastrous seventh grade experience?

In part, it was my attitude about Max. I never saw him as anything other than a successful writer, and I kept with him and at him the entire year, cajoling and encouraging, modeling and demanding, and explaining and expecting him to show up as a writer. Further, Max's success was due to his being on a team where students were encouraged to help one another; they worked in writing groups and shared reactions to one another's writing. Also, as with most writing assignments during the year, Max was allowed to select his magazine topic and thus honor his passion—skateboarding. When we legitimize the interests of kids and maintain an expectant attitude, we empower them to learn.

The National PTA®

For Elementary School Students

Give your children these great ideas for celebrating their teachers.

1. Make a bouquet of thanks.

    Your child can color and cut flowers out of paper, then write a word of thanks on each flower. Help her come up with words that compliment and best describe her teacher. Remind him of words that will make his teacher feel good, such as:

    > Thank you so much!
    > You're great! You taught me a lot!
    > You make school fun!
    > I'm glad you're my teacher!

2. Give a report card.

    Your child can make her teacher a thank-you card that looks like a report card. Include areas for "grading," such as:

    > Makes Class Fun
    > Helps Me Learn a Lot
    > Smiles Every Day

Grade teachers with the same phrases they use:

Super!

Great job!

Hard worker!

3. Do five nice things.

Your children can pledge to do five things, one each day, during Teacher Appreciation Week. Help them choose realistic activities, such as:

Help my teacher put away supplies.

Clean out a classroom closet.

Draw a special picture.

For Middle School Students

Your middle school student can appreciate his teacher with the following suggestions.

1. Design a thank-you card.

Write a note or poem about why she appreciates her teacher. She can design a special card or decorate her poem with pictures that show what her teacher has taught her.

2. Create a "Teacher Recipe."

For example:

1 cup of patience

1 tablespoon of fun

A pinch of courage

> Stir in a love for (science, music, literature) and
> Voilà, Ms. or Mr. Teacher!

Look at real recipes in cookbooks with your child to help him with the format for writing a recipe. Once the teacher recipe is complete, your child can present it tied to a bag of homemade cookies or muffins.

3. Plan a school assembly.

   For a real show-stopping tribute, children can work with parents (and the PTA), school staff, and fellow students to plan a show that honors teachers. Parents can work with groups of middle school students to write, direct, and act out skits that portray:

   > A typical day in the life of a teacher
   > School without teachers

   It's sure to be an assembly filled with original, funny, and heart-warming scenes.

For High School Students

Here are three ways that your high schooler can make a teacher's day!

1. Write a poem.

   Teens are often embarrassed to speak in public or express themselves in person. Teacher Appreciation Week is the perfect time for students to have an "excuse" to thank teachers who have given them special attention or help by writing a note or poem.

2. Plant a reminder.

   A group of friends, a classroom, or a grade level (freshmen, sopho-mores, juniors, seniors) can work together to plant a tree, flowers, or shrubs to honor teachers and beautify school grounds during this week.

3. Start a Teacher Feature.

    Each week or month, display a teacher's picture in school, along with a profile on why he or she became a teacher. Report on his little-known hobbies or interests, include his philosophy of teaching, add any quotes he's famous for, and end with his thoughts on the future of education. You can also publish your Teacher Feature in the school newspaper.

For Parents

You and the teacher are working together to grow a great child. Here's how to show your thanks for a job well done.

1. Say Thanks.

    Take time to write a personal note to your child's teacher, thanking her for the time and effort she's given throughout the year.

2. Give a gift certificate.

    Teachers often spend their own money to buy classroom supplies and special teaching items. Present a teacher with a gift certificate to:

    A local stationery shop
    An office-supply store
    A bookstore

3. Lounge with flowers.

    Send flowers or a plant to the teacher's lounge in your school to celebrate all teachers.

4. Volunteer.

    Help out in the school or classroom during the week. Chaperone for the next field trip. Your involvement not only helps the teachers, but it benefits your children and you, as well. That's a three-for-one deal! Don't forget to "volunteer" at home and reinforce what's being taught in the classroom. Let teachers know you want to be involved!

The National PTA®

Parents Wish Teachers Would . . .

1. *Build students' self-esteem* by using praise generously when appropriate while avoiding ridicule and negative public criticism.

2. *Get to know your students.* Find out as much as you can about each child's needs, interests, and special talents as well as the way each child learns best.

3. *Communicate often and openly with parents.* Contact them early about academic or behavior problems, and be candid rather than defensive when discussing school problems.

4. *Assign meaningful homework on a regular basis* that helps children learn. Provide parents with direction on how they can work with their children to make the most out of homework activities.

5. *Set high academic standards for all students.* Expect all of them to learn, and help them to do so.

6. *Vary your teaching methods.* Make learning challenging and relevant to children and their world.

7. *Care about children,* since children learn best when taught by warm, friendly, caring, and enthusiastic teachers.

8. *Treat all children fairly,* and don't play favorites.

9. *Enforce a positive discipline code* based on clear and fair rules that are established at the beginning of each school year. Remember to reinforce positive classroom behavior rather than just punish negative actions.

10. *Encourage parent and family involvement* by reaching out to involve parents in their children's education. Show them how they can help their children at home. Remember that parents want to work with teachers to help their children do their best.

Teachers Wish Parents Would . . .

1. *Be involved.* Parent involvement helps students learn, improves schools, and helps teachers work with you to help your child succeed.

2. *Provide resources at home for learning.* Utilize your local library and have books and magazines available in your home. Read with your children each day.

3. *Set a good example.* Show your children by your own actions that you believe reading is both enjoyable and useful. Monitor television viewing and the use of videos and game systems.

4. *Encourage students to do their best in school.* Show students you

believe education is important and that you want your children to do their best.

5. *Value education and seek a balance between schoolwork and outside activities.* Emphasize your children's progress in developing the knowledge and skills they need to be successful in school and in life.

6. *Recognize factors that take a toll* on students' classroom performance.

7. *Consider the possible negative affects* of long hours at after-school jobs or in extracurricular activities. Work to maintain a balance between school responsibilities and outside commitments.

8. *View drinking and excessive partying as serious matters.* While most parents are concerned about drug abuse, some fail to recognize that alcohol, over-the-counter drugs, and common substances used as inhalants are the most frequently abused.

9. *Support school rules and goals.* Take care not to undermine school rules, discipline, or goals.

10. *Use pressure positively.* Encourage children to do their best, but don't pressure them by setting goals too high or by scheduling too many activities.

11. *Call teachers early if you think there's a problem,* so there is still time to solve it. Don't wait for teachers to call you.

12. *Accept your responsibility as parents.* Don't expect the school and teachers to take over your obligations as parents. Teach children

self-discipline and respect for others at home—don't rely on teachers and schools to teach these basic behaviors and attitudes.

Enrichment for Students and Teachers

Alan Haskvitz

Student Enrichment

Career Exploration

Tech Prep

801 County Center III Court
Alpine Room
Modesto, CA 95355

Career brochures available, as well as additional information about ag education.

American Academy of Physician Assistants

950 North Washington Street
Alexandria, VA 22314

Free information on how to become a physician's assistant.

Computers

Microsoft

1-800-704-8215

Provides free workshops on Word, Excel, other Microsoft products.

Contests/Competitions

Computer Software Contest

720 Kuhlman Road
Houston, TX 77024
713-467-7172

A contest for ages eight to fourteen for the best homework project completed using a computer.

ICI Doodle Contest

Box 7330
Stockton, CA 95267

"A Day in the Life of a Cedar Pencil" doodle contest.

Kids Hall of Fame

Box 9600
Washington, DC

Awards for outstanding student activists under age fifteen.

Mathcounts

1420 King Street
Alexandria, VA 22314

Provides free handbook for this math competition.

Nuclear Age Peace Foundation

1187 Coast Village Road, Suite 123
Santa Barbara, CA 93108

Essay contest on how conflicts have been resolved peacefully.

Vegetarian Resource Group

Box 1463
Baltimore, MD 21203

Award for essays about a vegetarian diet.

Hobbies

American Numismatic Association

818 North Cascade Avenue
Colorado Springs, CO 80903
1-800-367-9723

Great junior membership for collectors of coins.

Quill and Scroll Society

School of Journalism
University of Iowa
Iowa City, IA 52242

This is a society for journalism students.

American MENSA

2626 East 14th Street
Brooklyn, NY 11235

Promotes activities for students who have high IQs.

Scholarships

Chocolate Chips Ahoy Challenge

Box 8122
Easton, MD

Show ways to demonstrate there are at least 1,000 chocolate chips in every 18-ounce bag and win a $25,000 scholarship.

Duracell-NSTA Scholarship

National Science Teachers Association
1840 Wilson Boulevard
Arlington, VA 22201-3000

Ocean Spray Company

1-800-662-3263

Scholarships for women athletes.

U.S. Department of Education

600 Independence Avenue SW
Washington, DC 20202

Free software to help students apply for federal student financial aid—a must for all high school administrators. Ask for FAFSA Express.

Wal-mart Scholarships

W-MSI
702 Southwest 8th Street
Bentonville, AR 72716-9002

Awards 240 scholarships.

Women's Sports Foundation

1-800-227-3988

Female athletes can win $1,000 from Mervyn's department stores.

Special Interest

ATT Toll Free 800 Directory

295 North Maple Ave. Room 5237A3
Basking Ridge, NJ 07920

Great source to help students with research.

Barbara Bush Foundation for Family Literacy

1112 16th Street NW, Suite 340
Washington, DC 20036

Parents and students learn together.

Center for the Book

Library of Congress
1010 Independence Avenue SE
Washington, DC 20540-4920

Library has guides for children's reading.

The Experiment in International Living

Kipling Road
Brattleboro, VT 05301

For those interested in foreign exchange programs, this program arranges exchanges.

I Have a Dream, Too!

http://www.inform.umd.edu/MDK-12/homepers/emag/dream.html

This Web site invites you to share a short essay or poem about dreams.

What are your dreams for yourself, your family, your community, your world?

Merriam Webster On-line!

http://www.m-w.com/

This site provides a free dictionary, thesaurus, and word-of-the-day email services.

The President of the United States

The White House
1600 Pennsylvania Avenue NW
Washington, DC 20500
202-456-7639

Tell the president—or the White House operator—your views. Free posters, pictures, and insights into White House layout and architecture are also available.

Sign Writing

http://www.signwriting.org/

Learn how to read, write, and type signed languages.

Trucker Buddy International

1-800-MY BUDDY

Students learn about travel by corresponding with truckers.

Who Owns What?

http://www.people.virginia.edu/%7
Edev-pros/Realestate.html

Here is an interesting resource that can be fun. You can check on property ownership practically anywhere.

Word Dance

http://www.worddance.com/

Word Dance magazine encourages the love of reading and writing in a nonthreatening, playful environment. It was created to give young people a quality vehicle for creative expression, a place where their voices can be heard.

Young Entomologists Society

Department of Entomology
Michigan State University
East Lansing, MI 48824-1115

For those who enjoy insects.

Sports

American Heart Association "Jump Rope for Heart" program

1-800-AHA-USA1

Call for free jump ropes and lessons.

League of American Wheelmen
6707 Whitestone Road, Suite 209
Baltimore, MD 21207

Information for bike riders.

United States Olympic Committee
One Olympic Plaza
Colorado Springs, CO 80909-5760

They have Share the Olympic Dream (800-423-5789) for $12.95. Best is their "Inside the Olympic Movement" pamphlet, which is in quick question-and-answer format. The back of the pamphlet has an excellent directory and calendar, so that students can write to their favorite group.

Teacher Enrichment

American Council of Exercise
1-800-825-3636, ext. #723

Free fitness program for fourth graders called Energy2Burn. Trainers come to the school to work with the children.

American Educational Research Association
1230 17th Street NW
Washington, DC 20036-3078

Get your free copy of the Educational Evaluation and Policy Analysis.

American Folklife Center
Library of Congress
Washington, DC 20540-8100

This is the national center for services to state-based folklife programs. Get "A Teacher's Guide to Folklife Resources"—a single copy is free for K–12 teachers.

American School Counselor Association
http://www.schoolcounselor.org/

The American School Counselor Association is the national organization that represents the profession of school counseling. ASCA focuses on providing professional development, enhancing school counseling programs, and researching effective school counseling practices.

America Taking Action
http://www.americatakingaction.com/

A national network of school Web sites.

Barbara Bush Foundation for Family Literacy
1112 16th Street NW, Suite 340
Washington, DC 20036

Teaches parents and students how to learn together.

Big World

Box 21

Coraopolis, PA 15108

Send $1.01 and a 9-x-12 envelope for a sample magazine on traveling inexpensively and off the tourist beat.

Caring Connections

Box 3867

Ballwin, MO 63022-3867

A free program for special needs children.

Canadian Content Site 21 C-50

Gabriola, BC V0R 1X0

Get a free copy detailing Canadian history.

Career Explorer

http://cx.bridges.com/

CX is a comprehensive library of career-related articles packaged as a daily magazine. It delivers independently researched job profiles, labor market analysis, and career development tools to more than 3,300 schools every day. Nearly 9 million page views were recorded on the Web site's national and regional CX services in 1998.

A Celebration of Culture—A Food Guide for Teachers

1-800-827-0833

1-800-827-0860

Call for a booklet on meal patterns and foods of the Vietnamese, Chinese, Filipino, Black, Korean, Japanese, and Latino populations.

Center for Folklife Programs and Cultural Studies

Smithsonian Institution

Attn: Betty Belanus

955 L'Enfant Plaza SW, Suite 2600

Washington, DC 20506

The center provides a nationwide list of scholars of various cultures. Also ask for a copy of the community scholar survey. You can write a letter asking if a volunteer can address your class.

Center for Living Democracy

RR#1, Black Fox Road

Brattleboro, VT 05301

Get their free newsletter filled with good features and products. They are also expanding into video and need good stories. Training workshops, learning center, TV series.

Center for Science in the Public Interest

1875 Connecticut Avenue NW, Suite 300

Washington, DC 20009-5728

Nutritional nuggets and other health information, including Nutrition Action newsletter and CHOW, a curriculum for nutrition.

The Chlorine Chemistry Council

http://c3.org/

1300 Wilson Boulevard

Arlington, VA 22209

Many free classroom materials and a video on introducing basic chemistry and the periodic table to students.

Danforth Foundation

231 Bemiston Avenue, Suite 1080

St. Louis, MO 63105-1996

Provides grants for schools wanting to improve.

The Department of Education Hotline

1-800-USA LEARN

Provides free newsletter, "Community Update," as well as free copies of U.S. Department of Education program, "Preparing Your Child for College." Areas each have their own regional contact. Also get the catalog at

almanac@inet.ed.gov; write "Send Catalog" in subject area. For a list of additional resources, get "A Teacher's Guide to the U.S. Department of Education."

Earthwatch Fellowships

Education Awards Manager

680 Mt. Auburn Street, Box 9104

Watertown, MA 02272

Provides funding for K–12 teachers to participate in two-week field research trips throughout the world.

Facing History, Facing Ourselves

15 Hurd Road

Brookline, MA 02146

or

25 Kennard Road

Brookline, MA 02146

A listing of classes and resource materials on the Holocaust. Videos are very interesting.

Federal Reserve Bank of New York

Public Information

33 Liberty Street

New York, NY 10045

Free materials and classroom sets of comic books on many phases of banking, money, and credit. Get "The Basics of Foreign Trade and Exchange." Also the "Story of Checks and Electronic Payments," a 24-page comic book, is a great way to teach economic principles. Free classroom sets.

Federal Reserve Bank of San Francisco

Public Information
101 Market Street
San Francisco, CA 94125

Free videos to explain economics as well as a vast amount of other free material. "Muffin Market" is a free supply-and-demand video that contains a computer program and a valuable lesson on economics. Check out the "Arithmetic of Interest Rates," weekly newsletters, and other materials.

Federal Reserve Bank of St. Louis

Box 442
St. Louis, MO 63166
www.stls.frb.org

The Money Tree, a curriculum package for grades four through eight about the role of money and banks. There may be a $25 charge for materials. Also get "Inside the Vault," a newsletter.

Field Trip Planning

http://curry.edschool.virginia.edu/curry/class/Museums/Teacher_Guide

Here you can learn how to plan your museum field trips more effectively.

Foundation of America

3020 Children's Way, MC 5093
San Diego, CA 92123
http://www.youthlink.org/

Free discussion guides to help students compare the issues and discuss the elections.

Friends Committee on National Legislation

245 Second Street NE
Washington, DC 20002-5795
fcnl@igc.apc.org

Get on their mailing list. Interesting political insights from the smoke-filled rooms. Get the Congressional Registry, which lists all committees and important phone numbers. You can get great tax charts for your students to use.

George F. Cram Co., Inc.

Box 426
Indianapolis, IN 46206

Awards for K–12 teachers for exemplary

classroom presentations about geography. Run by the National Council for Geographic Education.

The Giraffe Project

Box 759
Langley, WA 98260
http://www.giraffe.org.

This is an organization that recognizes people who stick their necks out to help others. Write them for story based K-12 curriculum that teaches courageous compassion and active citizenship.

Handbook of the Renaissance

2130 Carleton Street
Berkeley, CA 94704-3214

Lee McCray has the best Renaissance book in the business.

Intel

2200 Mission College Boulevard
Box 58119
Santa Clara, CA 95052-8119
1-800-346-3029
http://www.intel.com/**

Get *The Journey Inside: The Computer,* an absolutely fabulous resource that explains how a computer works. It has overheads, teacher's guide, video, chips, and batteries. A gift from the electronic gods.

Kaplan's

http://www.kaplan.com/

Kaplan's interactive site offers advice on tests, college admissions, student life, and careers, the Amazing College Simulator, Tuition Impossible, and The Career Hotseat.

Kidsphere

c/o Robert Carlitz
University of Pittsburgh
Pittsburgh, PA 15260
kidsphere-request@vms.cis.pitt.edu

Kidsphere is an Internet-based discussion groups for teachers who work on collaborative projects. It also hosts KIDs, which allows kids to write to other kids.

Kodak

http://kodak.com/country/US/en/di gital/edu/k12Solutions/index.shtml

This is the educator page from Kodak. It includes free lesson plans on photography and other materials.

Lions Club International

1-800-747-4448

Ask for their free kit on student volunteering entitled "The Future Is Ours . . . So Now What?"

Maurice Robinson National Mini-Grant Program

Constitutional Rights Foundation
601 South Kingsley Drive
Los Angeles, CA 90005

About thirty grants, each from $400 to $600 or more, to aid students in solving serious community issues.

Met Life Health and Safety Education

One Madison Avenue
New York, NY 10010-3690

Free video helps kids learn how to handle peer pressure.

Microsoft

1-800-704-8215

Provides free workshops on Word, Excel, and other Microsoft products.

NASA

c/o Annie Richardson
Radar Data Center
M/S 300-233, JPL
4800 Oak Grove Drive
Pasadena, CA 91190

SIR-C Education Program: free CD-ROM with radar images, shuttle photos, and lessons.

National Agricultural Library

10301 Baltimore Boulevard
Beltsville, MD 20705-2351

Provides the Global Change Information Resource packets, as well as other data. The packets include a guide to information sources, chronology of global climate changes and global warming, and a greenhouse effect bibliography series.

National Archives

Trust Fund Board
Washington, DC 20408

Provides all the WWII resources you need to teach this topic. Small charges for excellent materials.

National Gallery of Art

Constitution and 6th Street NW
Washington, DC 20565

Loads of free films and cassettes. Get the catalog of art extension programs.

National Geographic Names Database

Chief Branch of Geographic Names, USGS
523 National Center
Reston, VA 22092

Information on the U.S. Geological Survey as well as the Geographic Names

Information System and database. It is an interesting place for students to learn about toponymy. They are very friendly.

National School Supply and Equipment Association (NSSEA)

8300 Colesville Road, Suite 250
Silver Spring, MD 20910
1-800-395-5550

Be Your Best Scholarship for professional development activities.

National Student/Parent Mock Election

225 West Oro Drive
Tucson, AZ 85737
1-800-230-3349
http://www.cnn.com/ALLPOLI-TICS/

This is a superior organization that has many benefits beyond voting information. Get their free materials and contact them for awards and ideas.

National Teachers Hall of Fame

1320 C of E Drive
Emporia, KS 66801
1-800-96-TEACH

Provides scholarships.

Native Speaker

International Schools Service
Staffing Department
Box 5910
Princeton, NJ 08543

Provides free listings of overseas jobs for teachers.

Office of Educational Research and Development

U.S. Department of Education
National Institute of Student
Achievement, Curriculum and
Assessment
555 New Jersey Avenue NW
Washington, DC 20208
800-222-4922

Order information on all content standards. Also free parental guides on homework, watching television, self-esteem, computers, performance assessment, *ERIC Review* magazine, "All About ERIC," and countless other free materials.

Office of Elementary and Secondary Education (OESE)

Smithsonian Institute
Art and Industries Bldg., Room
1163, MRC 402
Washington, DC 20560

The Smithsonian offers great-integrated teaching materials. Ask for a free subscription to "Art to Zoo." Also, inquire about "Beyond the Frame," a multicultural approach to art through the illustrations of social and cultural issues.

The Oregon-California Trails Association

Box 1019
524 South Osage Street
Independence, MO 64051-0519

An award for an outstanding teacher (all ages) of westward migration.

OSCY

909 Fourth Avenue
Seattle, WA 98104

Volunteer to teach English in Taiwan.

Penguin USA

375 Hudson
New York, NY 10014-3657

Provides free teaching guides for English teachers. Topics include Stephen King's short stories and Shakespeare's *King Lear,* among others.

The Political Graveyard

http://politicalgraveyard.com/

This web site has lots of U.S. political history and burial information.

The President of the United States

The White House
1600 Pennsylvania Avenue NW
Washington, DC 20500
202-456-7639
President@WhiteHouse. gov
Vice.president@WhiteHouse.gov
Congress@hr.House.gov

Tell the president—or the White House operator—your views. Free posters, pictures, and insights into White House layout and architecture.

Project Vote Smart

129 NW 4th Street, Suite 204
Corvallis, OR 97330
1-888-VOTE-SMART
http://www.vote-smart.org/

Provides booklets to help students learn the issues and evaluate candidate performances. A free copy of the "US Government Owner's Manual" is also available.

Reading is Fundamental

600 Maryland Avenue SW, Suite 600
Washington, DC 20024

Free books and reading contests. Also ask about volunteers/volunteering.

Shoah Visual History Foundation

1-800-661-2092

A sponsored program that records the personal accounts of people who survived the concentration camps.

Shriners

West Glenn Communications
1430 Broadway
New York, NY 10018
1-800-325-8677

Write or call for their free video, "Against the Odds," about overcoming disabilities.

SignWriting

http://www.signwriting.org/

Learn how to read, write, and type signed languages.

Teachers Helping Teachers

http://www.pacificnet.net/%7Eman del/index.html

Good resource for new teachers.

Teaching for Multiple Intelligences

c/o David Lazear
Illinois Renewal Institute
200 East Wood Street, Suite 200
Palatine, IL 60067

Get on the mailing list for free units of study on controversial issues.

TESOL Placement Bulletin

1600 Cameron Street, Suite 300
Alexandria, VA 22314-2751

For $20 you get six issues on where to find a job teaching English abroad as well as networking ideas.

Time Capsule

http://www.si.edu/scmre/teaching-time.html

This exercise introduces the basic steps in creating a time capsule from start to finish.

United Nations

Department of Information
New York, NY 10017

Some free materials on UN and world peace. Order "UN Teacher's Kit" that contains the "United Nations Family: A Selected Bibliography, Everyone's United Nations, Basic Facts about the United Nations," and a host of other valuable materials. They have great addresses for locating information and even Tobacco Free Day materials. Also get free copy of "Universal Declaration of Human Rights."

U.S. Department of Commerce

National Oceanic and Atmospheric
Administration
N/NGSI, Wallace, SSMC3 #9361
Silver Spring, MD 20910

Provides information about World War
II.

U.S. Department of Education

600 Independence Avenue SW
Washington, DC 20202

Free software to help students apply for
federal student financial aid—a must for
all high school administrators. Ask for
FAFSA Express.

U.S. Postal Service Literacy Initiatives

Corporate Relations, Room 10541
475 L'Enfant Plaza SW
Washington, DC 20260-3100

Get the Wee Deliver in School Postal
Service program, a great way to teach
youngsters about the postal system. Lots
of materials.

WW II Commemoration Committee

Attn: Fulfillments
1213 Jefferson Davis Highway
Crystal Highway 4, Suite 702
Arlington, VA 22202-4303

Provides a full array of great materials
on the war.

Books and Curricula by Contributors

Books by Contributors

Madonna Hanna

Fashionshowitis: A Guide to Fundraising Fashion Shows. Tacoma, WA: Hanna Publishing, 1999.

Mommy, Why Are My Eyes So Big? Tacoma, WA: Hanna Publishing, 1999.

Shelley Hrdlitschka

Beans on Toast. Victoria, B.C.: Orca Book Publishers, 1998.

Dancing Naked. Victoria, B.C.: Orca Book Publishers, 2001.

Disconnected. Victoria, B.C.: Orca Book Publishers, 1998.

Tangled Web. Victoria, B.C.: Orca Book Publishers, 1998.

Lois Mauch

The Badminton Bonanza. Durham, NC: Great Activities Publishing Co.

Flying Feet. Durham, NC: Great Activities Publishing Co.

Curricila by Contributors

Larry Bordeaux

Elizabethan Five-Act Design of Shakespeare's *Julius Caesar*

Sample Literature Unit for *Macbeth*
SAT Preparation Course

Dr.Gerard Brooker

The Young Playwrights Festival of Connecticut

Ross Burkhardt

Alternative Education Program
The Inquiry Process. Logan, IA: Perfection Learning, 1993.

Ms. Mac

Midget Digits. San Angelo, TX: Mac Publications, 1996.

Mary McGrann

Touch a Heart (co-author): A social/emotional curriculum that can be integrated across all subject areas to educate and heal the total child in a social context

Lois Mauch, Janelle Schumacher, Dr. Bradford Strand, Karen Roesler, and Dr. Donna Terbizan

The Fitness Education Pyramid

Pam Schmidt

Slithers: An enrichment mini-course about snakes

Hyla Swesnik

What's the Word? Dallas, TX: Vocabulary Enterprises, L.C., 1995.

For more information, please contact Conari Press: 800-695-8585.

T he National Education Association (NEA) has made it easy for us to write Congress and make federal funding of public education a national priority. Ask your senator and representative to work to make funding available for education:

http://capwiz.com/nea/home/

S pecial thanks to President Bob Chase and members of the National Education Association for lending their expertise and real-life experiences to this
project. I am thankful and appreciative of their spirit of giving.

Disney's American Teacher Awards is part of the Disney Learning Partner-
ship, a philanthropic initiative supporting innovative approaches to learning that
promote student success. I thank them for giving this project their support and
guidance so that several of their award-winning teachers—Joanna Gallagher,
Kimberly Stewart, and Carla Woyak—could share their knowledge and wisdom.

The National Parent-Teacher Association (PTA) is the largest volunteer
child-advocacy organization in the United States. A not-for-profit association of
parents, educators, students, and other citizens active in their schools and com-
munities, PTA is a leader in reminding our nation of its obligations to children.
PTA has nearly 6.5 million members working in 26,000 local chapters in all fifty
states, the District of Columbia, the U.S. Virgin Islands, and in the Department of
Defense schools in the Pacific and Europe. I give my thanks to the organization
for generously sharing information.

I extend my heartfelt thanks to the staff and current fifty members of the
National Teachers Hall of Fame (NTHF) for their enthusiasm and commitment
to elevate and support the teaching profession and for their ongoing efforts to
give back to education. The NTHF members model courage and integrity in both
their personal and professional lives. I commend the Hall of Fame organization
for its attempts to address the impending teacher shortage through educational

outreach efforts that both recruit and retain quality individuals in the nation's most important profession—teaching. Special thanks for facilitating the contributions of NTHF inductees Bob Coleman (1994), Francis Mustapha (1994), Alan Haskvitz (1997), Dr. Gerard T. Brooker (1998), Ross M. Burkhardt (1998), and Ron Poplau (1999).

Thanks to the Council of Chief State School Officers and Scholastic, Inc., for sponsoring the National Teacher of the Year Program, awarding outstanding teachers the recognition and honor they deserve. Through this program I discovered State Teachers of the Year Juley Harper, Robin Zeal (2001), Marilyn Lance (2000), Pam Schmidt, Lynne Ellis, Antonio Fierro (1997), and Cathy Priest (1996).

I am ever grateful for Alan Haskvitz's open and giving nature. Alan is a social studies teacher at Suzanne Middle School in Walnut Creek, California. In addition, he serves as a staff development presenter nationwide; an audiovisual evaluator and design consultant for the local county Department of Education; and a tutor to multicultural students in English and art. Alan's teaching career spans more than twenty years, and he has taught at every grade level and in every core subject. He has been selected as one of the nation's top teachers by eight organizations. He has also been recognized many times for his innovative teaching practices and has received the following recognitions, to name just a few:

> National Teachers Hall of Fame Inductee, 1997
> *Reader's Digest* Hero in Education
> *Learning* Magazine's Professional Best
> National Exemplary Teacher
> National Exemplary Program
> Campbell's 22 Best Teachers in America Award of Excellence
> Washington Medal, National Teacher Award, Freedom Foundation

Christa McAuliffe National Award

Robert Cherry International Award for Great Teachers

Leavey National Award for Private Enterprise Teaching in Economics

As a teacher, Haskvitz and his students work continuously to improve their school and community. As a mentor and department head, Haskvitz's curriculum increased CAP/CLAS test scores from the 22nd percentile to the 94th percentile, the largest gain in California history.

A very special thanks to Alan and the Horace Mann Companies for sharing "Reach Every Child"—the most wonderful and extensive resource guide a teacher, parent, or student could ever want. Since there are over 5,000 resources in his guide, I was not able to list every source. For further information visit *http://www.reacheverychild.com/*.

To Ron Poplau, a deeply felt thanks for developing a successful community service program for his students at Shawnee Mission High School in Kansas City, and his willingness to teach all of us how to be of service.

A very special thanks to my teachers who have made this book and my first three books, *The Courage to Give, Teens with the Courage to Give* and *America, September 11th: The Courage to Give* possible. Mary Jane Ryan—friend, mentor, and expert editor—continues to teach me every day. I thank all of the wonderful staff at Conari Press, Will Glennon, Brenda Knight, Suzanne Albertson, Leslie Berriman, Jenny Collins, Julie Kessler, Everton Lopez, Don McIlraith, Brain Reed, Rosie Levy, Heather McArthur, Leah Russell, Miginon Freeman, Claudia Smelser, Pam Suwinsky—for their encouragement, unique talents, and commitment to the courage to give philosophy. Thanks also extended to Karen Frost and Jim Levine.

Some of our best teachers in our lives are the obstacles thrown our way. When I was diagnosed with multiple sclerosis in 1991, I had a choice to let the disease consume my life or to embark upon a new journey. I am grateful for everyone who continues to help me along the way—my husband and best friend, Steve; our children, Melissa, Todd, and Michael; our parents, Sarah and Marvin, Maxine and Erwin; our sisters and brothers, nieces and nephews, and our friends. I humbly say thank you.

Jackie Waldman, a Dallas native, began her teaching career teaching special needs children in Dallas Public Schools.

Jackie was living the "perfect life" with three healthy children, a loving husband, and a thriving business when she discovered she had multiple sclerosis. Instead of dwelling on her physical pain, she used that energy to begin a new career in volunteerism. Jackie co-founded Dallas' Random Acts of Kindness™ Week. She has appeared twice on *Oprah!* Jackie was chosen by CNN as one of their Millennium Heroes. She is a recipient of the 1999 Girls, Inc., She Knows Where She's Going Award.

The author of three books, *The Courage to Give*, *Teens with the Courage to Give*, and *America, September 11th: The Courage to Give*. Jackie inspires others to give through volunteering—no matter what—and to discover that they, too, can triumph over tragedy to make a difference in the world.

She is sponsored by Biogen, Inc., a global biopharmaceutical company, to share her message at multiple sclerosis and medical conferences across the country.

Jackie lives in Dallas, Texas, with her husband, Steve of twenty-nine years, three children, Melissa, Todd, and Michael, and their miniature dachshund.

For more information about Jackie Waldman, volunteer opportunities, and the subject of her books, visit her Web site at:

http://www.couragetogive.com.

For speaking and workshop inquiries, please call 214-373-6267.

To Our Readers

Conari Press publishes books on topics ranging from spirituality, personal growth, and relationships to women's issues, parenting, and social issues. Our mission is to publish quality books that will make a difference in people's lives—how we feel about ourselves and how we relate to one another. We value integrity, compassion, and receptivity, both in the books we publish and in the way we do business.

As a member of the community, we donate our damaged books to nonprofit organizations, dedicate a portion of our proceeds from certain books to charitable causes, and continually look for new ways to use natural resources as wisely as possible.

Our readers are our most important resource, and we value your input, suggestions, and ideas about what you would like to see published. Please feel free to contact us, to request our latest book catalog, or to be added to our mailing list.

2550 Ninth Street, Suite 101
Berkeley, California 94710-2551
800-685-9595 • 510-649-7175
fax: 510-649-7190 • e-mail: conari@conari.com
www.conari.com